959.0
H44
1953

SOUTH VIETNAM

SOUTH CHINA SEA

SAIGON

0   50   100

A SHORT HISTORY OF
CAMBODIA

A SHORT HISTORY OF
CAMBODIA

FROM THE DAYS OF ANGKOR
TO THE PRESENT

MARTIN F. HERZ

FREDERICK A. PRAEGER
PUBLISHER
BOOKS THAT MATTER
64 UNIVERSITY PLACE · NEW YORK 3, N. Y.

*Published in Great Britain by
Atlantic Book Publishing Co. Ltd.
of 119 & 120 Chancery Lane, London*

*Distributed in Great Britain by
Stevens and Sons Limited of
119 & 120 Chancery Lane, London*

©
Frederick A. Praeger Inc., New York
1958

Table of Contents

Preface	7
1. The Death of Angkorean Civilization	11
2. A Backward Glance at the Khmer Empire	25
3. Decadence and Dismemberment	39
4. The French Protectorate	57
5. The Road to Independence	73
6. The Agony of Cambodian Democracy	97
7. Cambodia in the World Today	117
Bibliography	137
Index	139

Preface

THE traveler coming by automobile from Saigon to Phnom Penh, the capital of Cambodia, crosses the border in completely flat country near a place called Svay Rieng where a tongue of Cambodian territory juts out into South Viet Nam. There is no natural terrain feature to indicate the frontier. Yet there are a multitude of signs that one is leaving one civilization and entering another. The Cambodian huts stand on stilts whereas the Vietnamese huts are built on the ground. The Cambodian language is a monotone while Vietnamese is tonal, like the Chinese. In Cambodia the saffron-yellow cloaks of the Buddhist bonzes (monks) announce that one is entering a country of *Hinayana,* the ancient form of Buddhism. In this flat, alluvial country traversed by the mighty Mekong river, an invisible line indicates the boundary not only between two countries but between two worlds.

This boundary between the Indian and the Chinese civilizations has relentlessly moved westward during the last five hundred years. The entire present country of South Viet Nam was at one time inhabited by Cambodians and by the Chams, also a nation of Hindu civilization but one which perished almost without a trace. Further to the west, what today is Thailand was also at one time part of Cambodia. Angkor, the magnificent sunken city in the Cambodian jungle, was once the capital of a mighty empire which extended all the way from Burma to the South China Sea. Its history, what little is known of it, is replete with drama and perhaps with meaning for the present and for the future.

The origins of Cambodia are shrouded in mystery. Legend has it that an exiled Indian prince once came to its shores, where he fell in love with the daughter of the Snake King, married her, and founded a dynasty. There is some faint historical evidence that this prince may have been identical with a Brahman noble by the name of Kaundinya who is mentioned in Chinese accounts of a country called Funan, which was the predecessor of Cambodia. In any event, the union between the King and a snake goddess constitutes a central theme of Cambodian mythology, and the seven-headed snake, or *Naga*, is found depicted throughout the art of

Preface

the country as Cambodia's mother and protectress.

That India was the fountainhead of Cambodian culture there can be no doubt, although during long periods the contact between the two countries was interrupted and the Khmer (Cambodian) civilization at its height owed little to any other culture for its finest development. Cambodian civilization flourished particularly in the area around the Great Lake of the Tonle Sap into which the waters of the Mekong are backed up each year, resulting in inundations comparable to those of the Nile. It was in that fertile area that the city of Angkor was founded in the ninth century, that it flourished for perhaps six hundred years and then perished. The road from the halcyon days of Angkor to the present is the one that I have tried to trace here.

I have spent two years in Cambodia. During that period I was struck by the absence of a succinct history of the country—or, for that matter, of any history at all, whether it be in French or in English. There exists a great amount of learned literature about Angkor, almost exclusively in French with the single exception of the erudite book by Lawrence P. Briggs which is listed in the bibliography at the end of these pages. But Mr. Briggs suffered from knowing too much and his book is not satisfactory reading for laymen. Besides, it stops when, in my opinion, the history of Cambodia becomes most interesting.

The same is true of the studies by French archaeologists.

The present little volume is designed to fill this gap and to avoid the shortcomings of the learned literature mentioned above. It is, as will be readily apparent, anything but scholarly. It is short. It tries to bring the history of Cambodia up to date. And it is certainly unencumbered by an excess of knowledge, except for the very last chapter. Alone, the distressing but fascinating diplomatic history of the last years, which I experienced in Phnom Penh, would justify the writing of a separate volume. But there are limitations upon what can be written, and my profession does not permit me to spend much time in looking backward. A real history of Cambodia, which would do full justice to all the great men and events of its glorious past, still remains to be written.

M. F. H.

Tokyo, 1958.

1.

The Death of Angkorean Civilization

LITTLE is known about the fall of Angkor. In the late thirteenth century, Cambodia experienced a great flood, and the waters of the Great Lake crept up to the walls of Angkor Thom and finally poured into the city. According to legend, the King of Siam (Thailand) sent boats overland to help in the rescue of the King of Cambodia and of the precious idols and holy books of Angkor. So high did the waters rise at that time that the army of Champa, which was then occupying the southeastern fringe of Cambodia, had to abandon its conquest. The legend says that King Senaka, the ruling Cambodian monarch, died during this temporary abandonment of the capital. His son Sihanu finally returned to Angkor, ascended the throne and proceeded to rehabilitate the dikes and irrigation canals and otherwise to consolidate the administration of his country. Little is known about the reign of King Sihanu except this legendary story:

Sihanu was extremely fond of a certain kind of sweet cucumber which only one man in Cambodia knew how to grow. He finally decided that he wished to have all the sweet cucumbers the man could produce, and to this end he established a royal cucumber patch and appointed the gardener, whose name was T-Chay, to the honorific post of Chief of the Royal Cucumbers. When T-Chay complained that thieves occasionally stole some of the savory vegetables, King Sihanu gave him a spear and appointed him not only Chief but also Guardian of the Royal Cucumber Patch.

One night, the legend says, King Sihanu was seized by an uncontrollable craving for fresh sweet cucumbers, or else he may have conceived a sudden fear that thieves might be making off with some of them. Accompanied only by two female guards, he descended from the palace to the royal cucumber patch.

The night was dark. The trusty T-Chay saw an unknown man approach in the dead of night, raised his spear, took aim, and with a powerful thrust transfixed the King, killing him instantly. There was great wailing in the palace of Angkor Thom (or Eintapath, as it was then called). Soon the Royal Council convened to decide who should succeed the

The Death of Angkor

monarch. Finding no one else who surpassed the old King in virtue, sagacity and loyalty, they decided to elevate T-Chay, the Chief of the Royal Cucumbers, to the throne. Thus T-Chay became the next King of Cambodia. He married the daughter of the dead King Sihanu and founded a new dynasty.

The authenticity of this legend is in doubt. In fact, there is no record of even the existence of a King Sihanu. But there is usually some kernel of truth in such legends. If, as is probable, King Sihanu was identical with the King Jayavarman VIII of Cambodian history, then T-Chay became the King Indravarman III who ascended the throne around 1295. While there is some uncertainty about the manner in which he became King, it seems not only that Indravarman founded a new dynasty but that, more important, he was a follower of Hinayana (Little Vehicle) Buddhism. Recent research has shown that King Jayavarman VIII was not killed but abdicated in favor of his son-in-law, although he had a son of his own who had a legitimate claim to the throne. A stone inscription found at Banteay Srei shows that the old King even issued a proclamation congratulating the country on having exchanged a weak old ruler for a vigorous young one. According to another account, the legitimate crown prince made an unsuccessful attempt to eject the new King, but had the toes of his feet chopped off (which automatically disqualified him from the throne) and was cast into a dungeon. If these reports are true, it is not likely that the proclamation of Jayavarman VIII was issued of his own free will.

According to the historian Adhémard Leclère, the legend of Sihanu and T-Chay reflects, indeed, a palace revolution in the late thirteenth century, involving not the accidental killing of the old king by his gardener but rather a *coup d'état* led by a palace dignitary who carried the honorific title of Royal Gardener. Indravarman III was quite likely a leading exponent of the new Hinayanist religion. It is a fact that all kings of Cambodia after him have been Hinayana Buddhists. The advent of T-Chay, or Indravarman III, soon after the Great Flood, thus represents a turning point in Cambodian history. As will be seen, some historians establish a link between that revolution and the fall of Angkor.

The successive invasions of Cambodia by the Thais were undoubtedly an important factor in the evacuation of Angkor. Coming from the north, the Thais had come down into the fertile plains of the Menam valley, building up a new state which eventually separated Cambodia from contact with its cultural and spiritual fountainhead, India. It is known that the Thais first shook off Cambodian domination around 1220, then repeatedly invaded Cambodia, and eventually even stormed the capital city of Angkor. When the kings of Siam established their

The Death of Angkor

capital at Ayuthia, only 200 miles from the Cambodian capital, it was a challenge which the Cambodian kings found it prudent to evade. After Angkor was occupied by the Thais several times in the fifteenth century, the Cambodian kings transferred their capital to Phnom Penh (then called Chadomuk), from where it was later moved to Pursat, then to Lovek, then to Udong and finally back to Phnom Penh where it is today.

The date and manner in which Angkor was abandoned are not known because with the advent of the new dynasty the construction of temples ceased, and temple inscriptions are the principal source of information about the period. The theory has been advanced that for a long time, perhaps for as much as a century, the royal court of Cambodia had been the last refuge of Brahmanism in a country that had been gradually converted to Buddhism. Indeed, some of the earlier kings had been devotees of Mahayana (Greater Vehicle) Buddhism, and it is probable that the many-faced Bayon, the strangest of the temples in Angkor Thom, represents King Jayavarman VII in the form of a Bodhisattva (future Buddha).* Under Jayavarman VIII there seems to

---

* There is, of course, a great difference between Greater Vehicle (Mahayana) and Lesser Vehicle (Hinayana, now called Theravada) Buddhism. The former looks upon the Buddha as a redeemer to whom one can pray, and it considers that among the way stations to Buddhahood there is one just short of Nirvana which is occupied by Bodhisattvas, future Buddhas who can help the errant human souls in their

have been a sharp reversal to Brahmanism, accompanied by widespread destruction and defacement of Budddhist images. But the arrival in power of T-Chay seems to have represented not only the official advent of Hinayana Buddhism: quite possibly it was the first popular revolution in Cambodian history.

"The revolution," says Leclère, "must have been popular at least in the cities, consequently democratic, and in order to curry public favor the new King probably renounced certain royal privileges such as the tremendous temple-building enterprises, the road-building projects with forced labor . . . which had cost so much treasure, so much suffering, so much misery. Thus construction of the last temple then abuilding, Angkor Wat, was abandoned, for its sculptures are unfinished. . . . The new religion, moreover, probably disdained to finish an enterprise of the old, and the people themselves,

---

arduous upward path. Hinayana Buddhism is far more austere: To the believers of this religion, which today is practiced in Cambodia, Laos, Thailand, Burma and Ceylon, there is no easy path to Buddhahood. Buddha is not a God but only a teacher who has long since passed into Nirvana, leaving behind only his teachings as guideposts to eternity. There are no Bodhisattvas. Even the Buddha statues in the temples are reminders of the greatness of the master rather than objects of devotion, and the religion calls for meditation and good works and above all renunciation, rather than prayer, as the road to salvation. It can thus be seen that the Mahayana cult was quite compatible with the cult of kings, who could have themselves pictured as Bodhisattvas; whereas the Hinayana cult with its emphasis on austerity was less compatible with king-worship or the building of large and splendid temples.

The Death of Angkor

feeling themselves stronger and freer, refused to be press-ganged any longer. Thus began the decadence of Cambodian architecture at the same time as the decadence of Cambodian power." The provinces revolted, the King had to grant liberties to them, and the Buddhist revolution coincided with the secession of the tributary provinces.

Louis Finot, another historian, sees the decline of Cambodia as a more direct consequence of the Siamese invasions: "A cultured aristocracy of foreign origin covered with a brilliant but very thin surface the mass of the Cambodian population. While it is true that some foreign invasions do not mortally strike at a civilization, they can very well wipe out an élite . . . particularly if they are accompanied, as was then the custom in the Far East, by immense round-ups of prisoners. It is no doubt the disappearance of this thinking and industrious segment of the society which explains the sudden end of the Sanskrit language."

"As far as the people are concerned," continues Finot, "there is no reason to believe that they reacted strongly against the aggressors. Perhaps they even greeted them as liberators. Indeed, when one considers that they were forced not only to provide the labor for the gigantic constructions whose mass astounds the visitor even today, but also to furnish support for the innumerable temples that dotted the empire . . . then one can hardly doubt that after several centuries of such a regime the working population was decimated and ruined. It probably showed little ardor in defending the cause of these rapacious gods who indentured slaves and pressed taxes from the people, and it is not impossible that the systematic mutilations that one finds in the temples were the work of exasperated peasants.

"Moreover, the victor offered the vanquished a precious compensation: he brought a mild new religion whose doctrines, being perfectly suited to a tired and eroded people, offered a modest religion whose priests were pledged to poverty, who contented themselves with a straw roof and a handful of rice, and a moral religion whose precepts assured peace of the soul and social tranquillity. The Khmer (Cambodian) people, one may believe, accepted it without protest and put down with relief the crushing load of their glory."

The historian Lawrence P. Briggs puts forward an even more daring hypothesis: that revulsion against the old Brahmanic religion led to a sudden exodus from Angkor. He writes: "The only escape for the masses was in flight. The sudden and permanent movement of this immense mass of people, from one side of the kingdom to the other, shows the nature of this migration. Like a serpent shedding its skin, these descendants of the fabled Naga snake-princess left their weary past behind them and moved on to a far region where they were no longer

The Death of Angkor

haunted by a nightmare of temples. In the long and brilliant Angkor period, no scene enacted on its battlefields or carved upon the walls of it galleries is more dramatic than its close. The story is related by no chronicle, recorded by no inscription, pictured by no bas-relief; but its implication is clear: first the King and the surviving notables, and then the people, fled from the 'great and glorious capital' of Khmer civilization as if it were ridden with plague."

These theories are interesting, but they are based on no evidence whatsoever. What evidence is available indicates that the first Hinayana Buddhist king of Cambodia was securely on his throne in Angkor Thom when the only reliable chronicler of the period, the Chinese Chou Ta-kuan, visited the capital as part of a Mongol embassy at the very end of the thirteenth century. The country had recently endured a disastrous invasion by the Thais, and the reigning monarch was described as a usurper who had gained his throne with the help of the King's daughter (who, according to this reporter, had stolen the Sacred Sword, symbol of Kingship, from her father and brought it to her husband, thus making him King). There is no mention of a decline in the royal power; rather there was a strong army with many elephants, and the capital appears to have been as resplendent as ever. It was impressive even to a visitor from the then greatest power on earth.

A Short History of Cambodia

It is known that Cambodia suffered another and greater invasion from the Thais in the middle of the fifteenth century, when Angkor was certainly occupied and even a Siamese prince put on the throne of Cambodia. But the Cambodian army was still strong enough to eject the invaders, reconquer the capital and secure the frontier again. Invasions by the Chams to the east were also repeatedly beaten back. Another Chinese embassy appears to have visited Angkor around 1452, or about a century and a half after the official advent of Hinayana Buddhism. Little information exists on that period because there are no more stone inscriptions, and many of the documents kept by the royal family were destroyed when the Thais more than a century later stormed and burned the new Cambodian capital of Lovek in 1587. The decline and abandonment of Angkor can be explained by the repeated defeats and conquests at the hands of the Thais, but the fact that the cities and temples of Angkor could fall into almost complete oblivion is a mystery that has not yet been solved.

The very knowledge of Angkor receded from Cambodian consciousness as of the fifteenth century, when the written annals begin. "Everything afterwards," writes Leclère, "is like a new beginning, as though there were night before and day only afterward. The facts of the past sink into the most profound oblivion. Even the names of the

The Death of Angkor

kings, the names of the royal cities, and the most salient facts of history are forgotten." Sanskrit, the language of Brahmanism, is replaced by Pali, the language of Mahayana Buddhism. The stone inscriptions testifying to the glorious past are no longer understood. Precious steles, doubtless containing inscriptions that could have informed us of the Angkor civilization, are uprooted, broken, and thrown into the mud of temple ponds. In the place of history there are legends, but Cambodian and Thai legends become interchangeable and unreliable as sources for the historian. The burning of the archives in the sixteenth century did the rest. While a few Buddhist priests still lived and worshipped in Angkor Wat, the jungle closed in on the other temples and monuments, and what once had been the flourishing capital of a mighty empire became a sunken mystery deeply covered by tropical vegetation, inaccessible and almost completely forgotten.

From the very incomplete and inconclusive facts that have been assembled by historians, it seems that the advent of Little Vehicle Buddhism contributed to the decline of Cambodian power—although it should be remembered that it was also the religion of the conquering Thais, so that this factor is not likely to have been controlling. What ceased suddenly was the building activity, including the cutting of steles on which much of our historical knowledge of the period depends. Otherwise, Angkor seems to have continued as the Cambodian capital for well over a century after the revolution that marks a turning point in its history. There is no evidence that it was abandoned precipitously.

Nevertheless, there seems merit in the theory advanced by Finot that a "decapitation" of Cambodian culture by invading Thais may have sped the decline. Whether the entire cultural élite was carried off into Thailand or a part remained to be taken away by the King when he moved to Phnom Penh, it is certain that a city like Angkor Thom with its surrounding elaborate irrigation systems must have required a large corps of skilled administrators and technicians in order to function. It is quite likely that after the Thai conquests, and *a fortiori* after its abandonment by the Court, the city's services ceased to operate, the irrigation canals fell into disrepair, the temples were neglected, schooling was no longer provided for the children, commerce stopped, quite possibly epidemics broke out, the city lay open not only to renewed Thai conquests but also to marauding bands, and gradually the remaining population drifted away. The process may have taken centuries.

Angkor was not really "rediscovered" as some tourist guidebooks state. Its existence was dimly known, and the presence of a profusion of Buddhist relics in Angkor Wat dating from more recent centuries testifies that in any event that largest of the

The Death of Angkor

temples had not fallen into complete oblivion. Angkor Thom's existence was known, but the surrounding temples, many of them enormous, which cover an area of 200 square kilometers, were literally rediscovered—one of them (Banteay Srei) as recently as 1914. The first Westerner who brought a description of Angkor to the outside world was a French naturalist, Henri Mouhaut, who had heard about the sunken city and decided to visit it in 1860. He was astounded, as visitors still are today, by the splendor and might of what must have been a tremendously vital culture, a culture which at its apogee, between the tenth and thirteenth centuries, could rival that of any of the European cultures of the day.

French science deserves great credit not only for having dug the art treasures of Angkor out of the suffocating embrace of tropical jungle growth, but also for having reconstituted many of the temples that had become a mere jumble of stones. In a task that has lasted for generations and is not yet completed, the Ecole Française d'Extrème Orient has painstakingly reassembled these temples in work whose complexity is hard to imagine: the Bayon, for instance, appears to be not one temple but two erected on top of each other. To get a conception of the magnitude of the task, the visitor need only visit the Ta Prohm, one of the great outlying temples that has been left approximately in the state in which it was found. Here one can see how the roots of tropical trees, searching through the minutest cracks in the stones, could over the centuries burst them apart and tumble gigantic structures to the ground, smothering them under a tangle of tree trunks, roots, bushes, and vines. The history and purpose of some of these structures are still matters of debate among archeologists.

2.

A Backward Glance at the Khmer Empire

ALTHOUGH there is a fair amount of information available on the names of Cambodia's kings during the Angkor period and about their genealogical connections, the battles they fought and the temples they built themselves, almost nothing has come down to us about the arts and sciences—no manuscript, no painting, no implements, no non-religious art of any kind, nor even religious art other than what was hewn or sculptured in stone. This is due to the fact that in the humid tropical climate anything made of wood, parchment, or thread has long since disappeared. While in Egypt, for instance, the dry desert air permitted papyri, wall paintings, and relics of many kinds to come down to us after thousands of years, in Cambodia the rains, tropical vegetation, insects, and mildew have over the centuries disintegrated even the hardest woods. Today the visitor may pass through the gates of Angkor Thom, from which he can look down a road for almost one mile to the Bayon, which marked the center of the city, and all he will see is jungle. Yet what today is jungle must have been a teeming, pulsating city, must have included palaces, offices, places of entertainment, stables, bathing pools, inns, and military barracks, as well as dwellings of hundreds of thousands of freemen and slaves. Not the slightest trace is left: even the royal palace, which was built of wood, has disappeared, leaving behind only the magnificent stone-sculptured platform on which it was erected.

Yet what has remained is enough to astound and inspire. Nobody knows by what technical means the old Khmers hauled the enormous blocks of stone from the Phnom Koulen, some fifty miles away, to the building sites and how they were hoisted into place—for some of the stones weigh as much as four tons. The irrigation system of the area included two giant man-made reservoirs, one of them one by two kilometers in size that is now being used again for a modern irrigation system constructed with American aid and that will largely follow the traces left behind by the Khmers of over 500 years ago. No information has been preserved about Cambodian astronomy, but all temples are exactly oriented on east-west axes.

The Khmer Empire

We know nothing about Khmer medicine, except for the fact that according to an inscription in the Ta Prohm there were 102 hospitals in Cambodia at the time of King Jayavarman VII (today there are only sixteen although these, of course, are in a much smaller country). As for the purpose of the various temples, it had to be laboriously reconstructed since most of the statues in the sanctuaries had long since been destroyed or carried away.

It appears that all, or almost all, the monuments found in the Angkor area were Brahmanic temples which Kings of Cambodia devoted to themselves, for all the rulers of Angkor were deified upon death and assumed new names as gods when they departed from the earth. Most of the deities were apotheoses of the King in the form of Vishnu, Shiva, or a combination of both named Harihara. The temples, it seems, were places both of burial and worship, and upon the death of the King arrangements were made for their perpetual maintenance by priests, to whom entire villages were indentured to guarantee support of the cult. Because the steles erected in the temples told the stories of these kings, boasting about their accomplishments, a fair amount of information is available about the battles they won and how for centuries they first maintained and extended the empire against the Chams to the east and later, with diminishing success, against the

Thais to the west. At its height, the Cambodian empire included not only today's Cambodia but Cochinchina and Annam, most of Laos, almost all of today's Thailand, and perhaps also portions of Malaya and Burma.

Fortunately, there is available one fairly detailed description of the old Khmer capital, written by the Chinese official, Chou Ta-kuan, who has been mentioned earlier and who came to Angkor in 1295 with an embassy from the court of Timur Khan, the Mongol emperor of China. Timur's father, the great Khublai Khan, had defeated Burma and helped the Thais obtain their independence from Cambodia. He had encouraged Annam to make war against Cambodia and Champa, and had in 1283 sent a small Chinese or Mongol detachment into Cambodia to exact submission of the Kings of Angkor. But, in the words of Chou Ta-kuan, the Mongol force "did not return." The Chinese embassy thus had the purpose of negotiating what had not been obtained by force of arms, a Cambodian suzerainty under China. It appears to have been successfully concluded although the negotiations lasted very long, giving Chou Ta-kuan plentiful opportunity during an entire year to observe the life of the Cambodian capital.

Chou Ta-kuan describes the four-headed towers over the gates of Angkor Thom, which one can still see today, but he reports that the central tower of each gate was covered with gold. Near the center

The Khmer Empire

of the city, he reports, was a gold tower flanked by more than twenty stone towers (presumably the Bayon). On the east side (of the Bayon) was a bridge of gold, two gold lions (one on each side of the bridge), and eight gold Buddhas under stone chambers. "About a *li* [one-third mile] to the north of the tower of gold there is a tower of copper. . . . The palace, the official dwellings, and the houses of the nobles are all oriented to the east. The tiles of the private apartments are of lead; the others are of yellow earth. The piles of the bridges are enormous. Buddhas are sculptured and painted on them. The body of the buildings is magnificent. The long verandas, the covered corridors, are daring and irregular, without great symmetry" The council hall, where the King used to show himself (now called Royal Terrace), had gold window frames. "At right and left are square columns carrying forty to fifty mirrors ranged on the sides of the windows. Below are presented elephants [which are still visible today]. I have heard it said that inside the palace are many marvelous things; but the palace is strictly guarded and one cannot enter."

During Chou's stay at Angkor, the King left his palace four or five times, thus permitting the Chinese chronicler to give us a fairly detailed description. Fearing assassination (it must be remembered that this was probably Indravarman III, who had ejected the legitimate King, imprisoned the crown prince, and changed the court religion), "he never leaves the palace without being clad in armor, so that neither knives nor arrows can wound him. ... He wears a gold diadem, or also has the top knot surrounded with garlands of sweet-smelling flowers like jasmin. Around his neck he carries almost three pounds of pearls. On his wrists, ankles, and fingers he has bracelets and rings of gold encrusted with cat's eyes. He goes barefoot, and the soles of his feet as well as the palms of his hands are dyed red. Whenever he leaves the palace, he carries in his hand a sword of gold" (the *Preah Khan,* to this day the supreme Cambodian symbol of sovereignty). When he set out from the palace, he was preceded by the girls of the palace carrying utensils of gold and silver. Then followed goat carriages and horse carriages, all ornamented with gold. More than one hundred parasols were garnished with gold and had gold handles. Then followed the King, standing on an elephant whose tusks were enveloped in gold, holding in his hand the golden sword. He was surrounded by his bodyguard made up of palace girls carrying lances and shields, and by a cavalry guard mounted on horses and elephants."

The high functionaries, "councillors, generals and astronomers," were carried about in palanquins of different kinds according to their rank. The highest dignitaries used a palanquin with a litter of gold and four gold-handled parasols. The next had a lit-

The Khmer Empire

ter of gold and one gold-handled parasol. The lowest dignitaries had only a silver-handled parasol. A centurion received a silver tablet (a seal); a commander of a thousand, one in gold. In keeping with their new status, even some bonzes (Buddhist monks) carried gold or silver-handled parasols. Bonzes are accurately described thus: "They shave the head, wear yellow clothing and leave the right shoulder uncovered. For the lower part of the body, they wear a skirt of yellow cloth, and they go barefoot. Their temples . . . contain only one image, entirely similar to the Sakyamuni Buddha, which they call Po-lai (*Preah*). It is dressed in red. Made of clay, it is ornamented with vermilion and blue. The Buddhas of the towers are different and all cast in bronze. The bonzes make one meal a day, prepared in the family of a host; for in the temples there is no kitchen. The texts they recite are very numerous. All are composed of palm leaves, bound very regularly. On these leaves they write black characters, but as they use neither pencil nor ink, I do not know with what they write. . . The prince consults them in important matters of state."

Chou Ta-kuan reports the existence of a small Chinese minority of tradesmen which was self-administering—much as the Chinese minority in Cambodia is today. He also notes another custom which has survived to this time—the King himself received and adjudicated popular complaints, "including appeals even against insignificant administrative decisions." Trial was often by ordeal, as in medieval Europe. Punishments were severe and included fines, whipping, mutilation, and burial alive. Among the peculiar court customs was the annual collection of a jar of human gall, which was presented to the King. The gall bladder was supposed to be the seat of courage. (As a matter of fact, even in English the word gall still sometimes stands for audacity). The gall was mixed with wine and then drunk, or it was used to wash the heads of the King's elephants. According to the French Abbé Bouillevaux, this custom, which is attested also by writers on the histories of other countries of Indochina, particularly Champa, was still practiced in Cambodia in 1850. What makes it somewhat gruesome is that the gall had to be taken from living human beings: there was an annual "gall harvest" when it was not safe to go out on the streets of Angkor Thom at night. As for Cambodian astronomy, Chou gives little information except to state that the court astronomers knew how to calculate the eclipses of the sun and moon. In writing, the scribes used a sort of chalk on black-colored deer skins or parchments, writing from left to right as today. Slavery was widespread: only the poor had no slaves.

Agriculture was highly developed. Chou mentions the natural annual renewal of the soil by the

The Khmer Empire

floods of the Great Lake, and says that three or four crops were produced per year. He reports the existence of floating rice, the kind whose stem grows longer as the floods rise, keeping the grain above water sometimes as much as three yards from the ground. In addition to rice, there were onions, mustard, egg plants, melons, gourds, sugar cane, and taro. Fruits included oranges, pomegranates, peaches, bananas, letchis, plums, apricots, some of which grew wild. Salt was obtained by evaporation on the seashore, as today. Wine was made of sugar cane, honey, rice, and tree leaves. Domestic animals were small horses, sheep, goats, pigs, chicken, and geese. Fishing in the Great Lake was important. Large iguanas, turtles whose feet were eight or nine inches long, and shrimp which weighed a pound or more were used as food. "There are crocodiles as large as boats, which have four feet and are exactly like a dragon, but have no horns; their belly is very delicious." Among wild animals mentioned were the elephant, rhinoceros, tiger, panther, bear, wild cattle, wild horses, deer, goats, gibbon and monkeys of several kinds, as well as a multitude of birds. The lion was not found in Cambodia or elsewhere in Southeast Asia. It was, however, an important heraldic and ornamental device, and many stone lions are found in Angkor and the surrounding temples. The fact that no Cambodian had ever seen a lion in the flesh accounts for their strangely misshapen appearance.

The average Cambodian, then as today, lived in a straw hut, even within the precincts of the royal capital. He dressed simply—all, men and women alike, even the wives of the King, wore only a loin cloth. They ordinarily went naked above the waist, and, of course, barefoot. But apparently even low-ranking people wore gold rings and bracelets. "Men and women anoint themselves with perfumes composed of santal, musk, and other essential oils." The size and material of their houses depended on rank. High-ranking people could cover their roofs with tile; all others used thatch (*paillote*). Sexual morality was, by Chinese standards, appalling: "The women of this country are said to be very lustful. One or two days after their confinement, they unite with their husbands. If the husband does not respond, he is abandoned. If the husband is called away on business, all goes well for some nights. But, after ten nights, the wife is sure to say: 'I am not as a spirit. How can I sleep alone?'. Thus, their depravation goes up to this point. But I have heard that certain ones keep faith." Homosexuality appears to have been rampant. As for sanitation, the houses had, of course, no sewage disposal. The Chinese visitor writes: "By two or three families they dig a ditch which they cover again with grass. When it is filled, they cover it over and dig another one. After having

The Khmer Empire

gone to this place, they go to the pond and wash themselves with the left hand, for the right hand is reserved for food. When they see the Chinese use paper, they mock them and close their doors. There are also women who urinate standing. It is ridiculous."

Chou Ta-kuan describes many domestic customs, including those attending childbirth and the rite which he calls *chen-t'an*, the deflowering of girls when they reach a certain age, a custom found also in Champa. "At an age between seven and nine years for rich girls, sometimes not before eleven for poor girls, a Buddhist or Taoist [probably Brahman] priest is charged to deflower them. . . . Each year the mandarin chooses a day in the month which corresponds to the fourth Chinese month and notifies all the country. Each family with a daughter subject to *chen-t'an* notifies the mandarin. The mandarin sends a candle on which a mark is made. At nightfall of the appointed day, the candle is lighted and when it burns up to the mark, the moment of *chen-t'an* has arrived. Some time before this date the parents choose a Buddhist or Taoist priest, to suit their taste or convenience. Certain ones have a regular clientele. Bonzes of some fame are preferred by the functionaries and the rich. The poor have no choice. Presents, according to the circumstances or generosity of the family, are made to these bonzes of wine, rice, cloth, silk, areca nuts, silver objects. . . . There are priests who refuse silver and accomplish the *chen-t'an* with poor girls. This is called a good deed. A bonze can deflower only one girl in one year."

As to the actual ceremony, Chou Ta-kuan trails off into uncertainty and indefiniteness. He reports that "on the evening of the *chen-t'an* a great banquet is organized, with music, and the parents and neighbors gather together. . . . That evening, with palanquins, parasols and music, the priest is brought. Two pavilions are constructed, of silks of various colors. The girl sits in one, the bonze in the other. No one can understand what is said. The noise of the music is deafening. I have heard it said that at the appointed time the bonze enters the girl's pavilion, deflowers her with his hand and then soaks his hand in wine. Some say that then the father and mother, the relatives and the neighbors all mark their foreheads with it. Some say they also taste it. Some believe also that the bonze really unites with the girl. Others do not. A Chinese cannot easily witness these things, so the exact truth is not known. When the day dawns, the bonze is taken away, with palanquins, parasols, and music. After that the girl must be purchased from the bonze with cloths and silks. If not, she remains his property and cannot marry another."

Although at the time of Chou's visit Cambodia had only recently been attacked and ravaged by the Siamese, it is obvious that the state was still

The Khmer Empire

prosperous and far from decadent. What few stone inscriptions are available from the fourteenth and fifteenth century also testify to a reduced, but still powerful state. Outlying provinces and vassal states had been lost but Kambujadesa, the mother country, was still intact despite the occasional invasions from the west. What had stopped was the construction of enormous monuments. The culture was one of conservation and reproduction rather than of new initiatives. The religion made for softer living, and with declining revenue the armies were presumably smaller and less well maintained.

According to the annals of Ayuthia, the Siamese invaded Cambodia in 1350 and took many prisoners, although they do not seem to have captured Angkor. But the city was captured in 1431, and on that occasion the annals of Ayuthia speak of statues and images carried away by the conquerors. The King of Siam placed his son on the throne of Angkor, but that ruler was shortly thereafter assassinated and the Cambodian heir apparent, Ponha Yat, reoccupied the capital. It was during this time of troubles that the King seems to have removed himself from Angkor. After the brief and colorful glimpse provided by Chou Ta-kuan no further account exists of the appearance and life of the Cambodian capital. A curtain of darkness gradually descended upon Angkor and the entire Khmer civilization.

3.

Decadence and Dismemberment

THE period between the abandonment of Angkor and the advent of the French protectorate, which covers 400 years of gradual decay, can only be understood against the larger background of the centuries-long clash between Indian and Chinese civilizations in Southeast Asia. Today Cambodia stands at the border between the Indian and Chinese cultures, but a thousand years ago it was still at the center of a great arc of Hindu kingdoms, among which the mightiest was Java, which for a time had subjugated Cambodia itself. (According to an Arab chronicler of the tenth century, a King of Cambodia had once rashly expressed the wish to see the head of the Maharaja of Java before him on a platter. The Maharaja heard of this, quickly outfitted a fleet, sailed up the Mekong, surprised the King of Cambodia, defeated him in battle, had him killed and decapitated, and upon his return to Java sent the head, pickled in a jar, back to Cambodia as a warning symbol of Javanese overlordship. King Jayavarman II, the founder of Angkor, was also the liberator of Cambodia from Javanese vassalage.) To the east of Cambodia, on that part of the Indochinese coast that later was known as Annam, there was another great country of Hindu culture, the kingdom of Champa which has already been mentioned.

The history of Champa, one of the many countries in the world that have completely disappeared as the result of foreign conquest, is replete with meaning to the student of Southeast Asia. Champa did not have the good luck of Cambodia, which was gradually encroached upon by two powerful neighbors and finally fought over and kept in being precisely because their rival claims tended to cancel each other out. Champa was located between the hammer and the anvil. Today, as the result of French scholarship and particularly due to the existence of Chinese and Annamite annals, we know a great deal about the history of Champa. Too often historians are tempted to reason fallaciously that because a country was wiped out, it must have become decadent or lacking in the warlike virtues. The Chams, according to all accounts, were a flourishing kingdom, they were versed in the Hindu arts and sciences, they had great leaders, they were hardy

Decadence and Dismemberment

and extraordinarily valorous soldiers. The gradual pattern of their defeat becomes apparent only over the centuries, for they often carried the fighting far to the north, into Annam and right up to the borders of China, and even after the most crushing defeats they again and again managed to rise and liberate themselves. But the secular weight of over-populated Annam, a country of Chinese civilization, kept pressing down upon them until in the end it wiped them out.

Champa was Cambodia's flank protection against the weight of Annamite pressure from the north, but in the politics of the day there can have been little awareness of that fact. To the Cambodians, the Chams (inhabiting what today is the northern half of South Viet Nam) were the closer rival and enemy, and Cambodia thus often combined against them with the more distant power, Annam (then inhabiting what today is North Viet Nam). As a result, after a struggle lasting for centuries, the Annamites not only overran Champa but finally poured into underpopulated Eastern Cambodia, absorbing province after province and gradually driving out Cambodian culture. The process was a gradual one which became accelerated toward the end, in the seventeenth and eighteenth centuries when Annam, having digested Champa, combined with Thailand in tearing off great chunks of Cambodia. As late as 1700, Saigon was still a Cambodian village. In fact, all of what today is known as Cochinchina, or the southern half of South Viet Nam, was once inhabited only by Cambodians. But today the Cambodians in Cochinchina are a small minority "with full rights as Vietnamese citizens" but by that token denied even minority status.

The pressure against the Indian civilizations of Southeast Asia was exerted from three directions. To the west of Cambodia, the Chinese and later the Mongols pressed down upon Burma and Siam. As we have seen, the Thais, coming from the mountain area of southern China, poured into the Menam valley, absorbed Cambodian Hindu culture, built up their own state, then liberated themselves from Cambodian vassalage, and finally became conquerors and occupiers of Cambodia. To the east of Cambodia, the Annamites pressed down from Tonkin, for centuries warred against Champa, finally absorbed it and in the end settled all of that part of old Cambodia that later became the principal part of South Viet Nam. Meanwhile, farther to the south, Arab Moslems made their appearance at the Straits of Malacca in the thirteenth century. (Marco Polo was among the first to report on the presence of "Saracens" in Malaya.) The empire of Java, after many vicissitudes, among which was a disastrous Mongol invasion by sea at the end of the thirteenth century, lost its hegemony over the other islands and then came gradually under the spell of Moslem

Decadence and Dismemberment

civilization, until today only Bali is a last refuge of the erstwhile Hindu culture in Indonesia. Thus in the space of a few hundred years, Cambodia, once at the center of an Indian world in Southeast Asia, became the outpost against the tide of Chinese civilization which it is today.

The real turning point of Cambodian history, according to this analysis, must therefore not be placed at the time of the abandonment of Angkor but at 1471 when the neighboring state of Champa was decisively crushed by the Annamites. Barely three generations before, in 1407, Champa had profited from Chinese annexation of Annam to recover its lost provinces, including its erstwhile capital of Indrapura which had been abandoned to Annam already around the year 1000. But in 1428 Annam succeeded in freeing itself again from Chinese domination, and the resurgent Dai Viet (as the Annamites called themselves) fell upon Champa with redoubled fury, taking its new capital Vijaya in 1446, then falling back before a Cham counteroffensive, but finally entering the Cham capital definitely in 1471. The Chams had sent desperate pleas for help to Phnom Penh, but the Cambodian ruler of the time appears to have been too busy with internal dissension (there were two rival kings holding portions of the country) and in any event too preoccupied with the Thai threat from the west to bother much about the fate of Cambodia's neighbor to the east. Thus the Annamites stormed and destroyed Vijaya, killed some 60,000 people and took 30,000 prisoners, including the King of Champa and virtually the entire royal family. With Champa henceforth reduced to a tiny principality vegetating in the area of Cap Varella, Annam now became a new and ever more powerful neighbor of Cambodia.

The effects were not felt for some time. The Cambodian King Ang Chan and his son Barom Racha managed in fact during the sixteenth century to inflict a number of defeats on the Thais, not being troubled much as yet by the surge of Annamite power on their flank. Ang Chan, upon his accession, refused the customary tribute of a white elephant to the King of Siam, and when the Siamese attacked in 1510 he inflicted a major defeat upon them, repeating the performance in 1524 when Cambodia's western neighbor made another attempt to reconquer the country. Ang Chan founded a new Cambodian capital at Lovek, where he is supposed to have built himself a magnificent palace—but since it was built of wood, nothing of it remains. When the Burmese invaded Siam and captured its capital Ayuthia in 1556, the Cambodian King Barom Racha profited from that opportunity to invade Siam the following year, and, according to the Cambodian annals, he took some 70,000 prisoners and regained several of the lost provinces. Barom Racha again campaigned successfully against Siam in 1559 and

Decadence and Dismemberment

1562. It can thus be seen once more that Cambodia was a far from decadent country after the fall of Angkor. Its decline was gradual and interspersed with many glorious episodes, like the decline of Champa.

The new Cambodian capital of Lovek was stormed and burned by the Siamese in 1587, and according to Henri Russier it is from that date that one should really reckon the period of decadence. As the reasons for that disaster, Russier cites two fatal mistakes by Sotha I, the King who succeeded Barom Racha. The first mistake was that Sotha listened to Siamese appeals for help against the Burmese. In 1568 Siam, with Cambodian help, managed to eject the Burmese invaders, but this only revived the Siamese threat to Cambodia itself. The second error was that Sotha I, weary with the cares of being King, abdicated from the throne and installed his eight-year-old son Chey Chettah as successor. The resulting internal dissension provided the pretext and opportunity for a new Siamese invasion "with 100,000 men, 800 elephants and 1,850 horses," resulting in renewed amputation of Cambodia's western provinces and a prolonged siege of Lovek which at first, however, was beaten off.

A Cambodian legend ascribes the final taking of Lovek to a Siamese strategem. Finding themselves unable to capture the new Cambodian capital in their first invasion because of a dense bamboo thicket

45

protecting the palisades around the city, the Siamese fired bullets of silver against the walls from all sides, making them fall short and thus into the bamboo thicket. Then they lifted the siege and departed. The Cambodians, finding that the Siamese bullets were of silver, thereupon eagerly sought them out and, in order better to find them, cleared off the bamboo thicket that had protected the city. Then the Siamese returned, found themselves better able to storm the palisades and breastworks, poured into the city, sacked it, and put it to the torch. A magnificent royal library, containing no doubt important relics from the Angkorean period, was also burned, although some of the art treasures and documents were taken to Ayuthia by the invaders, and later to Bangkok.

According to Cambodian accounts, the King managed to make his escape to Laos, but according to the annals of Thailand the King of Siam, after the capture of Lovek, "bathed his feet in the blood of the King of Cambodia" as he had vowed he would do when he embarked upon his campaign. This humiliating episode still rankles with the Cambodians. Only in 1956, Cambodian newspapers violently objected to publication in a Thai newspaper of a picture portraying the King of Siam laving his feet with the blood of his defeated Cambodian foe.

The next Cambodian King, Soriyopor, was crowned only in 1613, after he had reigned for thir-

Decadence and Dismemberment

teen years, which suggests that during that period the country was under Thai occupation. He abdicated in favor of his son, Chey Chettah II, who established friendly relations with Cambodia's new neighbor to the east and even married a daughter of the Emperor of Annam. He was the first Cambodian King to play the Annamites against the Siamese. With the help of his father-in-law, he managed to beat off two Siamese attempts to reoccupy Cambodia, but in return for the help of Annam he had to concede it the right to send settlers into the Saigon area. Chey Chettah II died in 1625 and, since his son Ponha To was still a minor, the country came under a regency of the young King's uncle, Outey. According to the Cambodian annals, as related by Leclère, young Ponha To eloped with his uncle's wife "on a trip to Angkor Wat" and was pursued by the regent and put to death together with the unfaithful woman. The episode is cited because it demonstrates once more that Angkor could not have fallen into complete oblivion after its abandonment as the old Khmer capital.

Under the succeeding kings, the influx of Cham refugees fleeing from Annamite persecution became a problem, impairing both internal Cambodian stability and relations with neighboring Annam. The latter intervened, the Siamese followed suit, and there ensued a period of internal and foreign violence in which some four or five kings disputed the Cambodian throne while attempting to rally the people against two foreign invaders. Of the leading rivals, one (Chey Chettah IV) was finally supported by the Siamese, the other (Ang Non II) by the Annamites; and as a result the country was for a time split, with one King residing at Udong, about twenty miles north of Phnom Penh, and the other at Saigon.

The Annamite-supported King, with some additional Chinese support, invaded the Siamese-supported part of the country, which roughly corresponded to today's Cambodia, on four occasions: in 1683, 1684, 1689, and 1691, but each time he was beaten off by the forces of King Chey Chettah IV and his allies, or rather protectors, Having finally reconquered all the Annamite-held areas, Chey Chettah IV abdicated in 1695 in favor of his nephew and became a bonze. However, his nephew died and he was forced to return to the throne. Three years later he abdicated again, this time in favor of his son-in-law, Ang Em, but the latter abdicated in turn two years afterwards, forcing Chey Chettah IV to become king for the third time.

These vicissitudes encouraged the Annamites to invade Cambodia once more, and this time with greater success. Udong fell as the result of treason; Chey Chettah IV was forced to flee, but he rallied his forces and managed in the end to drive out the invaders. However, this time he was not able to re-

Decadence and Dismemberment

store the old frontiers: Annam retained not only Saigon but a strip of territory reaching all around the Mekong estuary and up to Ha Tien on the Gulf of Siam, close to the present Cambodian-Vietnamese boundary. Having once more saved the nation, Chey Chettah IV abdicated yet another time, in favor of his son Thommo Racha II, aged only twelve. However, since the son proved too young to govern, Chey Chettah IV returned still another time to the throne, but after four years he relinquished the crown and sacred sword for the fourth and final time.

King Chey Chettah IV seems one of the most colorful kings of Cambodian history. His repeated renunciations, which tempt one to dub him the Great Abdicator, recall the actions of a more recent Cambodian King who earned the country its independence, then abdicated, took the premiership, resigned, took it again, resigned it again, took it yet another time and gave it up almost immediately afterwards. If more recent experience is a guide, the renunciations of Chey Chettah IV and his resumptions of office do not necessarily indicate that he wished to shed the duties of kingship at all cost. They may instead indicate an ambivalent attitude toward power, a desire to be rid of it, coupled with a belief (which may well have been justified) that he was the only man capable of holding the country together and defending its interests against foreign encroachment. One may speculate that the court of the Kings of Cambodia may have been riven by rivalries, factionalism, inefficiency, and corruption which paralyzed government except during the periods when Chey Chettah IV himself was at the helm, although it is not impossible that even during the times when he was in retirement in a Buddhist pagoda he may nevertheless have continued to hold the reins of the country in his own hands.

By the end of the eighteenth century, Cambodia was reduced to about half its size at the time of the abandonment of Angkor. There is little profit in enumerating the dynastic changes, invasions, counter-invasions, rebellions, and submissions. When in 1767 Ayuthia was once more captured and sacked by the Burmese, the Annamites had their great opportunity, and if they did not annex all of Cambodia it was only due to the historical accident that the Tay-Son rebellion broke out in their country at about the same time. Even so, by 1800 Annam had annexed and, what is more, settled all of Cochinchina with Vietnamese, to whom were now added Chinese refugees from Manchu domination. As Siam recovered its former strength, the Kings of Cambodia came to be crowned in Bangkok; but when this resulted in greater hostility from the Annamites, they for a time offered tribute both to Annam and Siam.

Decadence and Dismemberment

At the beginning of the nineteenth century, King Ang Chan revolted against the Siamese and fled to Saigon. Emperor Gia-Long of Annam sent him back to Cambodia at the head of an Annamite army which defeated the Siamese. But just as the Annamites had taken Saigon in "compensation" after their defeat by Chey Chettah IV, so the Siamese now detached the provinces of Battambang, Sisophon, and Angkor from Cambodia after their defeat by Ang Chan. The Cambodian victories, with foreign support, did no more than prevent the country from losing its identity completely, since neither of its more powerful neighbors desired the other to advance his borders too far. Nevertheless, the next Siamese invasion moved across all of Cambodia and into Cochinchina, and an Annamite counter-offensive later chased the Siamese back into their country.

When the Annamites thereupon in 1833 put King Ang Chan on the throne again, they finally left behind an army of occupation under their General Truon-minh-Giang; and when the King of Cambodia died in the following year, his daughter Ang Mey was put on the throne by the Annamites. She was queen not even in name, as her Vietnamese title, *ba-công-chua* (princess-mistress of life), indicated. She was widely reputed to be the *"sahay"* (a different kind of mistress) of General Giang, who ruled with an iron hand, gave Vietnamese names to the Cambodian provinces, and started to organize them on the Annamite pattern. Even the Cambodian dignitaries at the Court of Udong were required to dress and arrange their hair in the Vietnamese fashion. The nadir of Cambodian power had been reached. The erstwhile conquerors of Champa had become the conquerors of Cambodia. The tide of Chinese culture threatened completely to engulf the heirs of Angkor.

While Annam thus prepared to digest what remained of Cambodia, two potential pretenders to the throne still remained in the Siamese-occupied part of the country: Ang Em and Ang Duong, brothers of the deceased King Ang Chan. The Annamites managed to lure Ang Em to Pursat, where he was immediately greeted as liberator by the populace. Possibly because of the ominous character of these demonstrations, possibly because this had been their plan all along, the Annamites thereupon arrested Ang Em and shipped him off to Saigon. The atmosphere in Cambodia became highly charged. Soon thereafter, the Annamite general decided to ship off to Saigon the Queen herself as well as her principal advisers.

It is remarkable how quickly the news of all these doings spread throughout what remained of Cambodia. The Buddhist bonzes, whose religion was threatened with extinction by the Annamite

Decadence and Dismemberment

conquerors, helped organize the resistance. On a given day in 1842 the revolt broke out, and it resulted in a massacre of the Annamites wherever they were found. The revolt had no known head, it had only the hope of bringing back Ang Duong from Siam as a new King of Cambodia. Within eight days, small bands throughout Cambodia had cut all communications, overwhelmed the isolated garrisons, and beleaguered the cities in which the Annamites still held out. Revolutionary councils were set up throughout the country, and Cambodian dignitaries met and addressed a petition to the King of Thailand, asking him to intervene in Cambodia and place Prince Ang Duong on the throne. The Siamese did not hesitate long. They sent two armies, one overland and the other by sea.

The fighting that followed upon this episode —the ebb and flow of battles, the naval actions in the Gulf of Siam and the vicissitudes in the siege of Udong—are less interesting today than the basic lessons that flow from the Cambodian revolution of 1842. It was, first of all, a spontaneous popular revolution, organized by men of the people and coordinated by networks of messengers who gave cohesion to the actions of the peasants who had seemed (as they seem today) so compliant, dull-witted, and uninformed but who knew when their country's existence was at stake and responded to the supreme challenge. At the very end of the campaign, when all seemed lost as a fresh Annamite force took Phnom Penh and marched against Udong, it was not the Siamese army that won the victory but a bush army of Cambodian peasants that appeared from nowhere, routed the Annamites, and killed their general.

The second lesson, no less important, is that when the Cambodian people had to choose between an Annamite or a Siamese occupation, they chose the latter. To this day, Cambodians deeply distrust the Siamese, who are their cousins, but they passionately hate and fear the Vietnamese who are a world apart. Aside from all the ethnic, linguistic, religious, and other cultural differences, there was also a difference in the type of conquest: the Annamites colonized Cambodian soil, expelling the Cambodian peasants or harassing them to the point where they abandoned their land. The Siamese, on the other hand, while they annexed or occupied large portions of Cambodia, sent no settlers into them. On the contrary, they prevented the Cambodian peasants from leaving, so that those provinces could still be logically reclaimed when, many years later, Cambodia, with French help, was able to redress the balance of power.

King Ang Duong was crowned in 1847 on the basis of an agreement between Siam and Annam, an agreement that was facilitated by the timely death of the Annamite-supported pretender, Prince Ang

Decadence and Dismemberment

Em. The various members of the royal family held in Saigon and Bangkok were also returned, as was the sacred sword (*Preah Khan*) which had fallen into the hands of the Annamites and which was now enshrined in a special pavilion at Udong. In effect, the installation of Ang Duong restored not Cambodian sovereignty but rather Siamese overlordship by the consent of Annam and at the price of Cambodian acknowledgment of Annamite as well as Siamese suzerainty. Although Siam seemed to have the upper hand—the degree of Ang Duong's subordination is apparent from the fact that in 1848 he asked Bangkok's permission to name a new Prime Minister—the Annamites nevertheless made their pressure felt, particularly in slowly choking off Cambodian commercial contact with the outside world, which depended upon shipping on the Mekong.

Cambodia, devastated by over seven years of warfare, was economically prostrate. A plague epidemic decimated the capital city. Although King Ang Duong instituted a number of reforms and tried to rehabilitate his country, it was clear that he was at the mercy of his neighbors and that another war would finally wipe his country out. Under these circumstances, he cast about for protection from one of the European nations that had recently manifested their power in the Far East, and his choice fell upon France.

4.

The French Protectorate

KING Ang Duong did not, of course, have in mind the kind of protectorate that was later imposed upon Cambodia. He had in mind a French guarantee of his country's independence, in return for certain trade concessions. He sent a minister to Singapore to suggest such a treaty to the French consul there, but when the latter finally sent an emissary to Cambodia, the King of Siam heard about that mission and threatened Ang Duong with war if he signed any treaty with France. The Siamese overlordship would thus probably have continued if the French had not in 1859 defeated the Annamites and occupied Cochinchina, the part of Viet Nam that borders on Cambodia to the southeast. Ang Duong did not live to see the protectorate. He died in the same year and was succeeded by his son Norodom, but before the latter could be crowned a revolt broke out and he was forced to flee, first to Siamese-held Battambang and then to Bangkok, where he arrived with the royal insignia—the crown, sacred sword, and seal. In 1862, Norodom returned to Cambodia accompanied by Siamese troops, regained Udong, and installed himself there as King, although the Siamese prudently refused to send him his regalia until the situation had become stabilized.

King Norodom's position was thus weak, and it was rendered still weaker by the fact that France harbored in Saigon Prince Sivotha, the pretender to the Cambodian crown who had conducted the revolt of 1860. Moreover, France could claim co-suzerainty over Cambodia as successor to Annam. Various French representatives made this point in more or less friendly fashion, pointing to the protection they could offer against Siam. Finally, in 1863, a concrete proposition was put to the King by a special French emissary from Saigon, the now-famous Commander Doudart de Lagrée: the Emperor of France offered to "transform" into a protectorate the rights of suzerainty over Cambodia which he possessed as successor of the Emperor of Annam. A French resident would be assigned to the King of Cambodia, and Cambodia would agree to receive no consuls of other countries without the approval of France. French citizens would have the right to establish themselves freely in Cambodia,

The French Protectorate

and reciprocal rights were granted to Cambodians who might wish to establish themselves elsewhere in the French empire. In return, France would not only guarantee to protect Cambodia against external attack but would undertake also to "maintain order and peace in the kingdom"—which also meant that it would wash its hands of Prince Sivotha, the rival of Norodom. The draft treaty also provided for free entry of French goods and for extraterritorial courts to judge disputes between Frenchmen, whereas mixed courts would judge litigation between Frenchmen and Cambodians.

Faced with the choice of national extinction at the hands of the Siamese and this kind of protection offered by the French, Norodom signed; but the treaty first had to be sent to Paris for ratification by Emperor Napoleon III. In the meantime Siamese diplomacy applied severe pressure on Cambodia. The King of Siam not only threatened war but also called attention to the fact that he could withhold indefinitely the royal insignia which were still in Bangkok. Faced with these threats, Norodom signed a secret treaty with Siam recognizing the latter's suzerainty over Cambodia and ceding definitely the provinces which were under Siamese occupation. But as soon as the approved treaty returned from Paris, the French in turn applied pressure on Siam and finally obtained the dispatch of the royal insignia. King Norodom was thus crowned in 1864 with a crown that had been obtained for him by the French and that was in fact handed to him at the ceremony by the new French resident. Siam could still nominally claim suzerainty and was represented at the coronation by an ambassador, but he was prevailed upon to leave after the ceremony. French hegemony over Cambodia can thus be said to date from the crowning of King Norodom.

King Norodom was not initially a French puppet, but he eventually became one. The French protectorate established under his rule was not uncontested by the Cambodian people. Revolts broke out from 1866 to 1867 and again from 1885 to 1887, but they were finally put down by French troops in support of the Cambodian army, which at that time was led by the King's brother, Prince Sisowath. The country was divided. Action against the French implied disloyalty to the King, who was the symbol of the country's very existence. The French were hated, but as long as the royal court supported them, they could control the country with relative ease.

After the first insurrection was beaten down, the French moved to regularize relations with Siam which, naturally, had supported the rebels. They negotiated a treaty by which the King of Siam was made to renounce "for himself and his successors any tribute, present, or other sign of vassalage on the part of the King of Cambodia." In return, the Emperor of France promised not to incorporate

The French Protectorate

Cambodia into Cochinchina, which had meanwhile become a French colony, and recognized the definite possession by Siam of the provinces of Siemreap, Battambang, and Sisophon. This did not prevent France, however, from later negotiating new treaties by which those provinces were returned to Cambodia.

The protectorate became a virtual French colony in 1884 when King Norodom was forced to sign another document by which France assumed also control of the internal Cambodian administration. Under that treaty, the King undertook to "enact all the administrative, judicial, financial, and commercial reforms which the French government judges necessary in the interest of the protectorate." As a result, the entire Cambodian civil service was placed under the control of the resident. Frenchmen headed up the customs, internal revenue, postal, agricultural, forestry, health, veterinary, and other services, as well as the country's educational system. Residents and deputy residents were established in all the provincial capitals and other population centers, with all local Cambodian officials responsible to them through a Cambodian "mandarin" who was only nominally in charge. French troops were already established in the country, and to them was now added French control of the police. What distinguished the protectorate from a colony was essentially the institution of the royalty, which was still nominally the highest authority in the land. The French resident was an "advisor" to the King, but he had to have immediate access to the monarch, and the latter was obliged to accept his advice.

The overall record of the French protectorate, which lasted for almost ninety years, is difficult to assess, for there were many positive as well as negative aspects and these may well be given different weight by different observers. To allow the reader to form his own judgment, the accomplishments and liabilities of the protectorate will be enumerated below.

On the positive side, there can be no doubt that the protectorate kept Cambodia in being as a nation. Had it not been for French protection, the country would eventually have been swallowed up by Siam—indeed, had it not been for the French occupation of Cochinchina, Cambodia might have been earlier swallowed up by Annam or divided between the latter and Siam. As a second positive point, one must list the recovery of the lost provinces. As mentioned above, the French recognition of Siamese conquest in the treaty of 1867 did not prevent France later from exerting armed pressure on Siam to disgorge various border regions. By a treaty in 1904 and another one in 1907, France won back the provinces of Battambang, Sisophon, and Siemreap as well as certain territories in northeastern Cambodia that had been occupied by the Siam-

The French Protectorate

ese, all of which were reincorporated into Cambodia. Had it not been for the French, the great rice-growing area of western Cambodia, including the very ruins of Angkor, would today be located in an outlying province of Thailand. Further on the positive side, one must mention the remarkable work done by French science in exploring and recovering the past glory of Cambodia through the reconstruction and interpretation of the monuments of Angkor. Cambodia owes the awareness of its own historic grandeur to the French protecting power.

The French also deserve credit for their policy of exalting the monarchical institution, which today represents a key factor of national unity and stability. To be sure, French rule exploited the loyalty which Cambodians owed their King—indeed, as long as the people owed allegiance to the monarch and the latter was controlled by the French, the country could be governed with an economy of means—but in assessing the positive and negative aspects of French rule no distinction should be made between intentional and unintentional benefits or shortcomings. As it is, it must be set down as a remarkable accomplishment that the Kings of Cambodia, due to French policy, managed to retain their prestige and the allegiance of their subjects. The pomp and panoply surrounding the monarch were carefully maintained and respected. When the capital was moved from Udong to Phnom Penh in 1867, the King for a time lived in a palace that compared rather unfavorably with the French residence, but this was later corrected: the beautiful, authentically Cambodian royal palace which one may today admire in Phnom Penh, with its sweeping lines, its stacked gables, traditional ornaments, and profuse wall decorations, was designed by a French architect and constructed by the French in 1915.

A device by which the royal family was effectively enfeebled, even while outwardly unaffected in its prestige, was the manner in which the protecting power influenced the succession: instead of bestowing the crown upon one of King Norodom's sons, the French resident proposed to the Crown Council that the succession should go to the deceased King's brother Sisowath, who had been so helpful to the French in beating down the two rebellions. Sisowath reigned from 1904 to 1927, and his loyalty to France was such that Cambodians actually fought in the French army in Europe during World War I. (Khim Tit, who in 1956 was prime minister of Cambodia, had been a corporal in the French Army in 1918.) King Monivong, who succeeded Sisowath, was the latter's son, and his accession to the throne thus consecrated the existence of two rival royal lines, that of Norodom and that of Sisowath.

The kings led an easy existence devoted to art and to what, to Western eyes, seems like debauch-

The French Protectorate

ery but was in actual fact the expected conduct of Cambodian royalty. King Norodom still had some 200 wives, not counting concubines. The Sisowath branch was less wealthy (since Norodom passed his wealth to his children), thus more dependent on the French, but still able to maintain a sumptuous household. King Monivong still had some fifty wives, also not counting concubines. It was regarded as a signal honor to become a member of the royal ballet, and in Monivong's day all of those dancers were royal consorts.

After the death of King Monivong in 1941, the French were confronted with a difficult decision. The King's eldest son, Prince Monireth, appeared too independent-minded (and, indeed, independence-minded), so the French resident exerted his decisive influence on behalf of a younger member of the royal family who had the incidental merit of descending from both branches—Prince Sihanouk's father being a Norodom and his mother a Sisowath. Sihanouk seemed to the French to be more pliable, weak-willed, and accommodating. As is well known, they were mistaken in that appraisal.

Among the positive aspects of the French protectorate one may also mention the abolition of slavery, the strict division between executive and judiciary (the legislature was "consultative" and of no consequence), and the institution of an impartial system of justice which is still fondly and nostalgically remembered by Cambodians today. The civil administration was improved through the strengthening of the system of village headmen (*Mekhums*) who were given wide authority. A few hospitals were established. A fairly good road system was constructed. A railway was built from Phnom Penh to Battambang and thence to the Thai frontier. A small river port was constructed at Phnom Penh. City planning, both in the capital and in the provinces, deserves to be mentioned among the assets.

Economically, the country was not much developed except for the creation of rubber plantations, which were in effect French enclaves with foreign labor, contributing nothing to the economy but not draining out its substance. If economic development was scant, neither was there the rapacious type of colonialism found, for instance, in Dutch Indonesia. Cambodia under the French was a backwater, a rear area, a stepchild. Most of the French failures came from neglect rather than from exploitation.

The greatest French sin of omission concerned the field of education. An educated Cambodian élite might have aspired to high posts in the country's administration, but the kind of education that was provided stopped well short of preparation for university study. A senior high school was provided only in 1935, and the number of graduates from that institu-

The French Protectorate

tion (*"bacheliers"*) in 1939 was exactly four. There was, of course, no institution of higher learning in Cambodia, and Cambodians were discouraged from attending such institutions in France. Only one Cambodian obtained a medical doctor's degree in France before the war, and he was able to do so because he remained in France after enlisting in its army during World War I. Cambodia's only prewar graduate engineer, Sonn Voeunsai (at present in charge of the national railways), is the son of that doctor who, having resided in France, was able to overcome the obstacles in sending him there. Not a single Cambodian could study architecture, nor were any trained to qualify for leading positions in the various government departments such as agriculture, the postal service, public works, etc. By an accident, Cambodia had one man (Son Sann) whose family had been able to have him study at the Ecole des Hautes Etudes Commerciales in Paris and who thus had some qualifications to head the new National Bank when it was created in 1954. The dearth of trained executive talent is apalling.

University training of a sort was provided at the Indochinese University at Hanoi toward the very end of the protectorate, but no doctors were graduated there—only *"médecins,"* and their number was less than thirty in the case of Cambodians, proportionately much less than the number of Vietnamese. In the case of teachers, the record is even worse.

Only three Cambodians were trained in pedagogy at Hanoi and not a single one in France. Since there were no Cambodians trained to teach high school, almost all the teachers were provided by France, and to this day Cambodia is dependent upon French teachers for most of the high school training it provides. The bulk of primary education was left to the Buddhist pagodas. State-run primary schools numbered 107 (today there are 900) and, strangely enough, required the moppets to study French from the very first year. But the pyramid of education quickly became needle-shaped.

A few figures show the contrast between the regime under the French and under the present regime. In 1938/39 there were some 13,300 pupils in state elementary schools; in 1955/56 there were 195,100. On the next level (*"école complémentaire"*) the comparative figures are 3,200 and 57,100. In 1938/39 only 238 Cambodian elementary school teachers were graduated; in 1955/56 the figure was 7,146, not counting an additional 1,060 teachers trained in special accelerated courses which still could not meet the demand. Before the war, France devoted less than 8 percent of its Cambodian budget to education. Today, the proportion is over 20 percent, not counting foreign aid. Despite the enormous effort undertaken today, it will probably be a generation before Cambodia is able to obtain the necessary numbers of much-needed specialists in the many

The French Protectorate

fields required to run all government departments effectively.

For the sake of fairness, the French counter-argument to this record should also be stated. It is that Cambodians showed little interest in higher education during the protectorate, that pupils displayed a preference for the traditional pagoda schools over the new elementary schools, that much effort was required to make them attend the latter and that, in short, the supply of education seemed to meet the demand. In the case of doctors, also, it is stated that the number of dispensaries set up by the French seemed entirely adequate in view of the reluctance of Cambodians to be treated by European methods.

Most of these arguments are correct as far as they go, but if there was little pressure for higher education it was because young Cambodians knew that there would be no careers for them in their own country; if pupils stayed away from the French-run elementary schools it was because they were French-run; if high school students did not attempt to pursue their studies it was because graduation was made exceedingly difficult for them; if European-trained doctors were not sought after by the population it was because no effort was made to acquaint the people with the benefits of European medicine.

Even today the curriculum of the Cambodian high schools, with its emphasis on French history and the teaching of all subjects (except Cambodian) in an alien language, represents a strange phenomenon. However, it must also be stated that if the grade-school moppets soon forgot the little French they had learned in their first three years (which usually provided their entire schooling), thousands of other Cambodians have, thanks to their knowledge of French, had at least the possibility of communication with the outside world—when that communication became possible at the end of the protectorate.

It must be remembered that under the French regime there existed an entity called "Indochina," an artificial creation embodying today's Viet Nam (Tonkin, Annam and Cochinchina), Cambodia and Laos—an utterly anomalous entity that owed its existence only to French fiat and which has disappeared without a trace. The capitals of Indochina were Hanoi and Saigon, and it was normal—if one can speak of normalcy in the case of such an unnatural conglomeration—that customs, currency, and cultural and administrative services were concentrated in larger Vietnamese cities near the coast. This had a nefarious effect upon Cambodia: revenue from Cambodia was siphoned off for support of the services in Viet Nam; customs and currency offices were nonexistent in Cambodia; all trade was trans-shipped at Saigon and usually financed and controlled from there. What is worse, since trained Vietnamese officials in the offices in Hanoi and Saigon were familiar

The French Protectorate

with the overall administration of Indochina, it was natural that the French in Cambodia preferred to bring their Vietnamese assistants with them rather than train the under-educated Cambodians for such tasks.

The result was to intensify the inferiority of the Cambodians, and to make for an influx of foreigners across the nominal border separating Cambodia from Viet Nam. Today the French-imported Vietnamese administrators have departed from Cambodia, but there have been left behind some 300,000 other Vietnamese immigrants as well as some 250,000 Chinese who were brought or allowed in by the French. In the case of the Chinese, in particular, their establishment in Cambodia has resulted in almost all business activity being held in their hands. Desperate and only partly successful attempts are being made today by the Cambodian government to rectify that situation and to place at least part of the economic power into the hands of Cambodians.

There is involved here, as a matter of fact, a strange liability which arose from the relatively egalitarian character of Cambodian society. There never were large landowners in Cambodia. The society was a simple one, with the King originally owning all land, and with only a small class of "mandarins" or court dignitaries who could pretend to any status of wealth. This idyllic situation militated against Cambodia: whereas in Viet Nam there were wealthy merchants or estate owners who sent their sons to study in France and who gradually inserted themselves into the productive and administrative processes, in Cambodia there was little native wealth available for investment or capable of exerting socio-political influence. The most wealthy, enterprising, and gifted elements today are the Chinese, who now have a strangle-hold on import trade, banking, rice-milling, money-lending, bus transportation, and the distribution of almost all goods. This is a legacy of the protectorate that is full of perilous foreboding for the future of Cambodia.

5.

The Road to Independence

THE struggle for Cambodian independence from French domination was launched by Son Ngoc Thanh (pronounced *Son Nyok Tan*), a patriot who today leads a precarious existence in exile, fondly remembered by the men he once led but execrated as a traitor by the man who actually won Cambodian independence: King (now Prince) Norodom Sihanouk. The interaction between these two men is the story of Cambodia's struggle for freedom. There is grandeur in that story, and tragedy. It is, above all, a controversial story in which much right and wrong is to be found on both sides. Nobody can hope to tell it without giving offense to one side, or to both.

Son Ngoc Thanh founded in 1936 the first Cambodian-language newspaper, *"Nagaravatta"* (i.e.,

Angkor Wat), adopting this title so as to evoke memories of Cambodia's former greatness. "*Nagaravatta*" pursued an anti-French line which aroused sympathy among the younger members of the small semi-educated class and among some of the Buddhist monks, the former feeling a sense of frustration at their exclusion from any real power and the latter resenting the decline of their formerly great influence as a result of the introduction of Western ways of life. The anti-French tendency was vastly strengthened by the defeat of France and the occupation of Cambodia by the Japanese in 1941. Although the Japanese allowed the French to retain the civil authority, they permitted the Thais to take back the western provinces of Cambodia which the French had wrested from them in 1904 and 1907. Under such conditions, Cambodians were justified in asking themselves what value there was in the French protectorate. Instead of protecting Cambodia, the French administrators had become helpless puppets of the Japanese.

In 1942, Son Ngoc Thanh launched a revolt against the French, but the French police scotched his uprising, the Japanese support on which he had counted was not forthcoming, and he was forced to flee. His two principal associates in the revolt, Pach Chhoeun (pronounced *Pak Chun*) and a monk named Hem Cheao, were arrested. Thanh himself was given refuge in Japan. As the war continued

The Road to Independence

and Japanese fortunes declined, the French in Cambodia became restive and, as elsewhere in Indochina, planned a revolt of their own. However, the Japanese got wind of these plans and on March 9, 1945 they disarmed and interned all French forces throughout Indochina. Two days later, on March 11, Emperor Bao Dai proclaimed the independence of Viet Nam. On March 12, young King Sihanouk also proclaimed the independence of Cambodia. The Japanese thereupon brought back Son Ngoc Thanh who on June 1 was appointed Foreign Minister. Two months later, Thanh ordered the arrest of the other ministers and installed himself as Cambodia's first Prime Minister. His cabinet included Pach Chheoun, who had revived *"Nagaravatta"* after the Japanese freed him from a French prison.

    The capitulation of the Japanese in August 1945 left the Cambodian patriots without an army to oppose the return of the French. Son Ngoc Thanh announced his intention of maintaining Cambodia's independence and, in an attempt to bolster his position, organized a plebiscite in September in which the people voted overwhelmingly to support his independent government. However, he was not allowed to use this popular expression as a bargaining point with the allied occupation authorities as he had hoped. At the request of General Leclerc, Thanh was arrested in October by the British Brigadier Murray, Allied commander in Indochina south of the seventeenth parallel, and was sent to a French jail in Saigon and thence to exile in France. A Commissioner of the French Republic arrived in Phnom Penh, and King Sihanouk signed a proclamation denouncing Son Ngoc Thanh and proclaiming the loyalty of Cambodia to the French protecting power.

The French did not reestablish the protectorate in quite the manner in which it had existed before. On January 7, 1946 they signed a *modus vivendi* under which Cambodia was to be an "autonomous State within the French Union." Under that agreement, Cambodia was to govern itself but the Commissioner was required to "give his approval to legislative and regulatory texts and acts, to proclamations and circulars or instructions of general application as well as to decisions reserved, because of their importance, for the signature of His Majesty, the King." Although the *modus vivendi* spoke of ending the protectorate, most of the power was shifted to the fictitious Indochinese federation: a broad number of services (including large-scale public works, most judicial matters, the treasury, secondary and higher education, customs, mines, railroads, and foreign immigration) were regarded as "federal," coming under the control not of the Cambodians but of the French High Commissioner. A French military mission was to train Cambodian forces, but the French remained responsible for the direction of "public order." Foreign affairs were

The Road to Independence

controlled by the French government. It was essentially the old regime with some slight shifts of authority to the Cambodians. To sugar the pill, however, the French undertook to obtain the return of the western provinces which the Japanese had made them cede to Thailand in 1941, and this return was effected by the end of 1946.

King Sihanouk and his advisers were of the opinion that any further progress toward independence could be accomplished only by patient negotiation with the French, and the French encouraged this belief by proclaiming their readiness to negotiate. Given the utter weakness of Cambodia at the time, the King's attitude does not seem unreasonable. Moreover, there was the example of Viet Nam, which had appealed in vain to President Truman, Marshal Stalin, Prime Minister Attlee, General Chiang Kai-shek, and the United Nations against the reoccupation of Saigon by the French. The government of Ho Chi Minh, infinitely more powerful than had been the government of Son Ngoc Thanh, was still obliged in March, 1946 to allow French troops to enter Haiphong and Hanoi. Armed resistance to the French appeared out of the question for Cambodia.

Yet not all Cambodians felt that this was so. After the arrest of Son Ngoc Thanh, some patriots fled to Thailand and to the then still Thai-occupied western provinces of Cambodia, where they formed armed bands, calling themselves Khmer Issarak, or Free Cambodians. The Thai government probably hoped to use these dissidents as an instrument for preventing the re-establishment of French power in Cambodia, which might allow it to retain the ceded territories. Under the leadership of Pach Chhoeun, a Khmer Issarak committee was formed as a provisional government in exile. Armed clashes occurred along the Thai-Cambodian frontier, but the movement during this phase did not yet assume serious proportions. Pach Chhoeun himself surrendered to the Cambodian Government in April, 1946, and later in the year the surrender of the ceded territory by the Thais undermined the Khmer Issarak effort. As liberation by force of arms became more unlikely and the struggle for independence in Cambodia shifted to the parliamentary scene, many Issaraks availed themselves of an amnesty offered in April, 1947 and returned to swell the ranks of the Democratic Party. By the end of 1947, over 3,000 Khmer Issaraks had surrendered. Perhaps an equal number still remained under arms, in scattered bands, some of whom were no more than simple bandits.

The Khmer Issaraks were not the only dissident force under arms against the French. While these bands were active largely in western Cambodia, other bands, spilling over from Southern Viet Nam, were active in the eastern portion of Cambodia, basing themselves at first upon the Vietnamese set-

The Road to Independence

tlers in those parts. These were the Viet Minh, or Vietnamese freedom fighters who eventually became completely controlled by the Communists. During the early stage of sporadic fighting against the French in Cambodia, some Viet Minh established liaison with the Khmer Issaraks without necessarily distinguishing between their objectives. During this period, however, neither Issarak nor Viet Minh strength in Cambodia was substantial, and cooperation between the two, where it existed, had little political significance. Later, as the Communist character of the Viet Minh became apparent, the cleavage between them and the Issaraks became sharper, making them in the end overt rivals and enemies, although the French consistently tried to represent them as friends and allies.

The *modus vivendi* of 1946 was intended to be only a temporary stop-gap, but negotiations between the French and Cambodian governments dragged for almost four years before the next stage in Cambodian freedom was reached, and even this was attained principally because of the greater pressure in Viet Nam which had forced the French to grant a larger measure of independence to Bao Dai in March, 1949. The Franco-Cambodian treaty of November 8, 1949 was meant to give Cambodia "independence" without granting full sovereignty: Cambodia received an international personality and was allowed, as were the other "Associated States" of

Indochina, to establish its own foreign relations—but the accreditation of Cambodian diplomats was to require the concurrence of France. The fiction of the French Union was introduced, with an Assembly and a "High Council" which merely camouflaged French predominance. In the military field, Cambodia had to agree to the maintenance of French bases in peacetime and to French control of operations in wartime. In the field of the judiciary, mixed tribunals were to continue to judge Frenchmen (and even Chinese), and guarantees were written into the new treaty for French investments. In almost all internal fields, however, Cambodia obtained true freedom.

King Sihanouk and his Prime Minister, Yem Sambaur, attempted in vain to present this agreement as a Cambodian success and as the best which could be obtained—which it was, under the prevailing circumstances. The King offered another amnesty to the Issaraks, the French began another military campaign against them, and for a time it looked as though the situation might become stabilized. However, three factors prevented a consolidation. First, the Yem Sambaur government was a minority government maintained in power against the opposition of the Democrats, the majority party in Cambodia. That party, which had become the focal point of Cambodian nationalism, naturally attacked the treaty, and the Cambodian Parliament refused to ratify

The Road to Independence

it. Secondly, the French had suffered new reverses in Viet Nam and had been reluctant to furnish arms to the new Cambodian army, for fear that those arms might find their way to the Issaraks. Meanwhile, the Thai government fed arms to the Issaraks and perhaps also to the Viet Minh. Insecurity thus increased again. Thirdly, since the Cambodian Parliament consistently refused to ratify the treaty (indeed, at the time of its signature the National Assembly had just been dissolved), King Sihanouk attempted to place it in effect through a series of "protocols of application." In negotiating these protocols, the French thought it wise to water down the concessions they had made in the treaty, notably in the judicial field. This resulted in several successive governments refusing to sign the protocols, and a situation of juridical ambiguity was thus combined with the general malaise and dissatisfaction over the treaty and with continuing internal insecurity.

The French throughout this period attempted to operate through the King of Cambodia against his government and parliament. Their tactics were to play the government against the opposition and to picture the Democrats as enemies of the monarchy and the Issaraks as stooges of the Communists. Moreover, they had, of course, the power to remove the King and they were able to draw upon the support of well-informed advisers and experts in court intrigue. When the government of Yem Sambaur refused to sign a "provisional military accord" which would have confirmed French military control, they prevailed upon the King to dismiss the government.

To the King, it no doubt seemed that Cambodia was forced to rely on French power not only to preserve the monarchy but also, and principally, to protect the country against the growing threat of the Viet Minh. Yem Sambaur, on the other hand, expressed not only his opinion but also that of his enemies, the Democrats, when he declared in 1950 to a visiting journalist: "We can take care of the Issaraks without French help. If the country were really independent there would be no Issaraks. There would be no reason for them." However, he warned, French measures of indiscriminate repression would drive the Issaraks into the arms of the Viet Minh.

The same argument, however, could be turned around, and this is what the King did. While one could warn the French that their presence was encouraging the Issaraks, one could also warn the Issaraks that their activities furnished justification for the French military presence, that they divided the nation, that their activities were playing into the hands of the Vietnamese Communists (the Viet Minh) and that they endangered the only element that could hold Cambodia together: the monarchy. Such arguments, combined with a more substantial quid-pro-quo, succeeded in luring out of the jungle

The Road to Independence

the most important active freedom fighter of the time: Chhuon Mochulpich, who still today is known under his *nom-de-guerre* "Dap" (Corporal) Chhuon. This courageous and mystical leader, however, insisted on having his forces integrated into the Cambodian army while retaining full control of them, and up to this time he rules the province of Siemreap as a more or less private fief. Dap Chhuon's surrender was a major success for King Sihanouk and was used —fruitlessly—as an argument to prove to the French that the Cambodian army could handle the Issarak problem better than they.

In 1951 there occurred a dramatic change in the situation. New elections were held, and they resulted in a smashing victory for the Democrats. At the request of the new government, King Sihanouk obtained from the French the return of Son Ngoc Thanh. The arrival of Thanh at Phnom Penh produced an outbreak of nationalist frenzy which has never been seen in the capital either before or since: Over 100,00 people lined the road to the city from the airport at Pochentong. Thanh had become a symbol of the fight for complete independence and sovereignty, and his influence among the intelligentsia, the Buddhist clergy, the Army, and, of course, the Democratic Party was considerable.

Thanh never left any doubt that he felt there was only one policy to follow: to demand, insist upon, and, if necessary, fight for complete sovereign independence from the French. Soon after his return, he started publishing a newspaper called *"Khmer Krauk"* (Cambodian Awakening) with the help of his talented assistant, Ea Sichau. Publication of this paper still further inflamed the passions against the French, who soon came to see that they had made a mistake in allowing Son Ngoc Thanh to return. After they had in vain atempted to tar him with the Communist brush, they decided to arrest and deport him once more. However, Thanh was warned in time, and, together with Ea Sichau, made his way into the jungle to join the Issaraks.

Son Ngoc Thanh as an Issarak was a somewhat different man from Son Ngoc Thanh as Prime Minister or from the returning hero who had loyally conferred with and advised King Sihanouk: seeing himself once more denounced by the King and called a traitor, he did not hesitate to call the King himself a French puppet and to ventilate the possibility that Cambodia might be better off as a republic. Son Ngoc Thanh formed a Committee of National Liberation, and soon he breathed new life into the Issarak movement which, although in its heyday it probably didn't count more than 10,000 men, became a respectable military factor. It is a moot point whether the new committee ever entered into formal relations with the Viet Minh. In some cases, Thanh's men are known to have fought the Vietnamese

The Road to Independence

Communists and the Vietnamese- and Communist-inspired Cambodians who made up the Viet Minh.

To confuse matters, the Viet Minh on their part created a "Committee for the Liberation of the Cambodian People" and started to boost a leader whom nobody had seen before and whom they called Son Ngoc Minh, doubtless to capitalize upon the prestige of Thanh. Moreover, to compound confusion, Son Ngoc Minh headed up something called the "United Issarak Front." As usual, the Communists did everything to capitalize on a nationalist cause, to penetrate it, and to arrogate its leadership to themselves. Tragically, the French in Cambodia did much the same that the Germans had done in occupied France: by calling all resistance fighters Communists or stooges of the Communists, they did not reduce the prestige of the resistance but merely boosted that of the Communists.

The situation in Cambodia thus became very precarious. Public insecurity increased, and serious doubts existed whether the Issaraks were not being secretly aided by the new Cambodian army which was supposed to fight them. The young people, many Buddhist monks, and the majority party regarded the King as a puppet and sympathized with the resistance. In June, 1952 the King was obliged to fire the Democratic government, which had become completely intractable. He issued a proclamation asking for emergency powers for three years, during which period he undertook to obtain full independence.

The proclamation honestly pointed up the difference between the King and the Issaraks: "The Issaraks claim to be fighting for Cambodia," the King said, "and so do the Army and the police. As Son Ngoc Thanh has said, all Cambodians must join together on one side. Only, one has to agree on what side." The King added that he knew many people considered him a puppet interested only in the pleasures and advantages of his position and complained that some "looked him impertinently in the eye, particularly young people," who regard him as a useless and harmful dead weight . . . His conscience, however, was clear: "I say, on the other hand," he concluded, "that the so-called heroes have never done anything constructive, that they have only brought disorder, disuntiy, and ruin while shouting that France has not given real independence. They speak of public servants sucking the blood of the people, but they help themselves to the wealth of the country without any vote or control. If the Issaraks win, there will be unbridled arbitrariness. . . ." Thus spoke King Sihanouk on June 17, 1952.

Looking back with the benefit of historical hindsight, it can now be recognized that King Sihanouk was at that time seriously misjudged not only

The Road to Independence

by the Issaraks but also by the French. When the King dismissed the Democratic government he did so not only because he was at loggerheads with it but also because he was under extreme pressure—French tanks were patrolling Phnom Penh and the French Minister for Associated States, Jean Letourneau, had specifically declared that France would make no concession to a Democratic government. Having dismissed the government, the King now meant to obtain the concessions himself, and he was staking his entire future on that expectation. By the end of 1952, he came to the conclusion that he could only negotiate successfully if he provided evidence of controlling his own country.

The trend, however, was in the opposite direction. In January, 1953, a bomb exploded in a classroom of the French-run high school in Phnom Penh, the Lycée Sisowath, and a provincial governor was killed in ambush by the Viet Minh. A county chief was killed only twenty miles from Phnom Penh. Having in vain asked the National Assembly to pass a budget, to ratify the treaty of 1949 and to vote him emergency powers, the King dissolved that body on January 13, 1953. He declared martial law, had twelve Democratic deputies arrested, and incidentally suspended all members of the Cambodian Legation in Bangkok, which had apparently transmitted money and military information, received from Phnom Penh via the diplomatic pouch, directly to the Issaraks on the Thai-Cambodian border. In Phnom Penh, and in the provincial capitals, there was no longer any overt opposition either to the King or to the French. But more than three-fifths of Cambodia was in the hands of the Issaraks and the Viet Minh.

Almost immediately after his dismissal of the Assembly, King Sihanouk left Cambodia for "a month's vacation in Italy." Remembering that the King had been a playboy and that he had displayed only a fitful energy in politics, alternating great activity with periods of lethargy and even frivolousness, observers interpreted his European trip as new evidence that he was unstable and incapable of sustained effort. When he established himself at La Napoule, on the French Riviera, his enemies rejoiced, thinking that he was about to confirm what they had whispered about him.

However, King Sihanouk was only winding up for his big offensive. Before long, General de Langlade was to speak of the King as "running amuck," and the French magazine *Match* was to headline him as "The Mad King of Cambodia." (It was during the ensuing period that much information about his private life, about his saxophone-playing, love affairs, and movie-making was featured in the irate French press, leading some foreign journalists astray even today in their judgment of his personality, particularly when they are working for pub-

The Road to Independence

lications which maintain "background files.") But the King was deadly earnest, and he was entering, if one may use this Buddhist phrase, upon an entirely new incarnation. The Sihanouk of 1953 was a tough-minded man playing shrewdly for exceedingly high stakes. With the advice of his wily Prime Minister Penn Nouth and the young razor-sharp counselor Sam Sary, the King now entered the arena of international politics. He has not lost a single political battle, whether abroad or at home, since he embarked upon what he termed his own "Crusade for Independence."

King Sihanouk first sent a lengthy memorial to the President of France, in which he politely discussed, in his usual rather prolix manner, the reasons why Cambodia should forthwith be granted full independence. He pointed out that "the Issarak propaganda speaks of me as the principal obstacle to complete independence . . . they say that I and my government are too Francophile to make our country really sovereign. Now, I ask you, Mr. President, what am I to reply to this propaganda when I am denied the means to fight effectively to defend my people . . . ? What am I to reply when the Issarak propaganda points out to the people and to the clergy that Cambodia is not really independent since its King . . . has no power over the Frenchmen, Vietnamese, and Chinese living in the country?" Eighty percent of the Buddhist clergy, and a large part of the élite, of the government functionaries and of the students, he declared, were under the influence of the Issaraks. "I permit myself to think and to say that France must radically change her policy if she is not to betray her mission and the promises she has made to Cambodia . . . It seems to me that it is the duty and the self-interest of France to entrust to the Cambodians themselves the destiny of their country." The King adduced innumerable arguments, complaints, parallels and precedents, and ended by offering to come to Paris to discuss his demands.

King Sihanouk now refused to accept any more promises and would settle for nothing less than complete independence. There is irony in the fact that he used the danger from Son Ngoc Thanh and the Issaraks as his most effective argument, while continuing to excoriate Thanh himself and even lumping him with the Communists. ("The policy of France risks throwing the Cambodians into the arms of Son Ngoc Thanh, *i.e.* of the Communists," he could still write to the President of France.) Thanh could thus claim to have pushed Sihanouk into demanding full independence. The tragedy, on the other hand, is that even after the King had launched his own campaign for full independence, Thanh refused to support him but continued in dissidence right up to the present, ever suspecting his rival of knuckling under or

The Road to Independence

selling out to foreigners, until Thanh himself became a mere foreign-supported detractor and disgruntled politician living a precarious jungle existence on the border of Thailand, a disillusioned man who finally preferred the bitter bread of exile to a return to Cambodia where he would have to hear, day in and day out, his enemy Sihanouk extolled as the man who won the independence of his country.

The French government was exceedingly busy with a much more threatening situation in Northern Viet Nam and did not appreciate in time the urgings from King Sihanouk, whose presence on the Riviera gave rise to facile parallels with the activities of Bao Dai, the playboy Emperor of Viet Nam. His appeals were merely referred to the government, and although President Auriol invited him for lunch, this was followed by the issuance of a communiqué which merely highlighted the French reluctance to turn over full military authority to Cambodia. The Minister for Associated States said that the King's presence in Paris might be construed as "pressure" applied to the French government and suggested that he return to Cambodia. This the King interpreted as an outright snub. Instead of returning to Phnom Penh, he next showed up in Ottawa and then in New York, where he gave an interview in which he said that should the Viet Minh regulars invade Cambodia (they were then invading Laos), they would meet little resistance since the restrictions imposed by the French on the nation's autonomy deprived the existing regime of popular support and fostered the idea that the Viet Minh were struggling only for national independence. Next, the King flew to Tokyo. Arriving in Phnom Penh, he proclaimed his "Crusade for Independence" to cheering crowds from the palace balcony and almost immediately afterwards, to dramatize his struggle, departed for voluntary exile in Bangkok. Later he moved to Battambang in Western Cambodia, but he vowed not to return to the capital until he had achieved full national independence.

This escapade created great excitement. In Phnom Penh, the situation became so threatening that the French brought in additional troops to protect their own nationals and issued arms to their civilian residents. Obviously, something radical had to be done to meet the situation, and on July 3 the French offered to "complete the independence and sovereignty of the Associated States," but they again meant to conduct negotiations on how this was to be accomplished. The King replied by demanding immediate, complete and unconditional transfer of all authority in the military, political, monetary, economic, customs and judicial fields, offering only to allow the French to retain some garrisons and to give them favorable treatment in the economic field. Eventually, the French gave in on all the remaining points at issue. The last sticking point related to

The Road to Independence

Cambodian troops fighting under French command outside of Cambodia, but the French finally agreed to integrate these also into the Cambodian Army and to allow the King to take over the command in all areas still under French military control. The turn-over of military authority, although it was embodied only in one partial agreement, was construed by the Cambodians as the final granting of sovereignty. The King declared that independence had been attained, and on October 8, 1953 he re-entered Phnom Penh in triumph as the liberator of his country.

The granting of complete independence to Cambodia did not, however, end the war between the French and the Viet Minh, whose Vietnamese character thus became all the more apparent. Although Prime Minister Penn Nouth had proclaimed that Cambodia "does not have to oppose Communism unless the Communists seek to impose their doctrine on us by force," the Viet Minh invaded Cambodia toward the very end of the war, just before the Geneva Conference. These were not guerrillas but regular forces coming from North Viet Nam, and their eruption into Northeastern Cambodia did what neither the French nor the King had quite succeeded in doing: it made it plain for everyone in Cambodia that the Viet Minh were in fact Vietnamese invaders whose fight had nothing to do with the fight for Cambodian independence.

A Short History of Cambodia

At Geneva, the Communist powers still tried to elevate Son Ngoc Minh's "Liberation Committee" to the status of a Resistance Government and to claim representation for this "Government" in the conference, parallel to the representation accorded the Viet Minh. Son Ngoc Thanh also made an attempt to be heard. But the conference did not entertain either suggestion. The final agreement imposed on the Viet Minh the clear obligation to withdraw their forces from Cambodia, and when the armistice went into effect most of them actually departed. How Cambodia's attitude toward the Communists subsequently changed is related in another section.

After the Geneva conference, and benefiting from the amnesty which it decreed for all dissidents, Son Ngoc Thanh briefly came out of the jungle and attempted to re-enter the political arena. In November, 1954 he addressed a message to King Sihanouk, pledging his loyalty and requesting a royal audience. The news was not even published in Phnom Penh and became known only through the Indian and Thai radio stations. Had Son Ngoc Thanh simply proceeded to Phnom Penh, where the newly arrived International Control Commission would have protected him, he might have been able to re-establish himself gradually. But he had asked for a royal audience and, remembering Thanh's triumphal arrival in Phnom Penh three years earlier and his unwelcome advice, his request was not only turned

The Road to Independence

down but publicly denounced: "You would not serve His Majesty, the King at the critical hour when he was accomplishing his royal mission," the answer read, "but instead went into the bush to work against the King and to try to prevent him from accomplishing his mission. You have broken promises, you have openly attacked the King and his government, saying that they have done nothing but play a comedy to lull the people to sleep so that the French could oppress the Cambodians . . . If the Monarch had not obtained the independence of Cambodia, the people would have condemned him and his entourage to death, for you and your men have denounced them as traitors." All of which was, of course, completely correct.

6.

The Agony of Cambodian Democracy

DEMOCRACY, Western style, has not been a great success in Cambodia. However, it was not tried for very long, and the experiment took place under highly unfavorable conditions. As we have seen, the country was seething with unrest, and its struggle for independence became a domestic political issue in which the Parliament and the King developed differing conceptions of how the desired goal should be attained. In addition, the King and the majority party did not see eye-to-eye on how the country should be governed. In the end, Cambodia developed a special form of government which is altogether peculiar to itself. This is not surprising, for the personality of King (now Prince) Sihanouk is also unique, and the entire postwar history of Cambodia revolves around him.

The father of Cambodian democracy was Prince Yutevong, who died in 1947 at the age of thirty-four. He was also the founder of the Democratic Party and by all accounts a person of great idealism, persuasiveness and energy. Prince Yutevong, who had been educated in France, was a strong believer in civil liberties and parliamentary democracy as these concepts were then understood by the Left in France. The French administrators who were to assist him in the preparation of the new Cambodian constitution, however, were (as usual in Indochina) exponents of the Right, and the Right in France had rejected the new French constitution for giving excessive powers to the National Assembly. The French in Phnom Penh thus first proposed that Cambodia follow the Persian rather than the French model. Later they tried to limit the civil liberties granted by the new charter, and finally they made a sticking point of the "right of dissolution" which had been denied in the French constitution.

Prince Yutevong, however, pressed for the full extent of constitutional liberties enjoyed by France herself, with the result that the original Cambodian constitution had almost all the weaknesses of the French constitution—except in one respect: It does permit a government to ask the King to dissolve the National Assembly. Unfortunately, however, although in France such a provision would have been highly salutary, in Cambodia it provided no stability because differences arose not only between the government and the parliament but also between those bodies and the King, an eventuality which was never envisaged by the constitution-makers.

There is a certain magic, a kind of inherent dynamics in universal suffrage, which impels newly elected representatives of the people to try to exercise the very maximum of power in the people's name. The record of Cambodia is in this respect not different from that of many other countries. Hardly had the first Assembly, which was intended to be only "consultative," been elected by universal suffrage than it proceeded to ignore the protests of the French and of the King that it was supposed to consider only the draft constitution. Even before that constitution had gone into effect, the Consultative Assembly of 1946 discussed such subjects as an amnesty for the insurgents, although it technically had no right to do so. Exasperated, the pro-French prime minister, Prince Monireth, handed in the resignation of his cabinet, and Prince Yutevong, leader of the Democrats, became the first Premier responsible to an elected Cambodian body. He was also, however, the first Premier who had, perhaps unwittingly, placed the Parliament in opposition to the King.

The Democrats won fifty-four out of seventy-five seats in the elections of December, 1947. The

Liberal Party, which was somewhat more closely tied to the royal family, won the remaining twenty-one seats. The other parties which had emerged were completely unsuccessful, although their leaders were subsequently to obtain some prominence: neither the Khmer Renovation Party led by Nhiek Tioulong nor the National Party led by Khim Tit won any seats. It would be an exaggeration to say that there were clear-cut issues between the parties and that the people made an informed choice when they chose the Democratic Party to govern. All that can be said about that party is that it had from its very beginning the support and cooperation of the intelligentsia (*i.e.*, the high school graduates, most of whom were minor government officials) and that it was regarded as the best bet to obtain full independence. It was, of course, completely loyal to the Crown and was looked upon with favor by the Buddhist hierarchy which, as we have seen, had become an important nationalist force even though it played no overt role in politics.

It cannot be said that the first parliament worked in an orderly or efficient manner. Lack of experience in parliamentary practice and in the party system led to obstruction of business in the house and to frequent dissensions within the Democratic Party. The very first cabinet, headed by Chhean Vam, found its powers insufficient, asked for more, and was immediately overthrown on that issue. The next cabinet, headed by Penn Nouth, was soon overthrown on a corruption issue having to do with the granting of river fishing rights—an issue which in Cambodia always touches the lives of thousands of people because the privilege to build a fishing barrage across one or more branches of the Mekong or Tonle Sap rivers could deprive all fishermen down-stream of their livelihood. (The stringing of nets across an entire river was a capital offense in the old days of absolute monarchy.) Seizing on such a popular issue, a deputy named Yem Sambaur overthrew the government, seceded from the Democrats and formed a minority grouping. Yem Sambaur was an able political tactician. He felt he had public opinion with him and he obtained the confidence of the King, who designated him to succeed Penn Nouth.

Inexorably, the gap between King and Parliament thus widened. In designating Yem Sambaur, who represented only twelve deputies out of seventy-five, the King very likely chose the most able man, but it required much persuasion from him to make the Assembly give investiture—and the Democrats never forgave themselves afterwards for having been compliant. Yem Sambaur was a vigorous premier. He obtained certain concessions from the French and exposed corruption; but he was at continuous loggerheads with the Assembly. The majority party was jealous of Yem Sambaur's successes in his negotiations with the French and began to obstruct them. Some feared that he might become a dictator, and even elements close to the King distrusted the Premier because of his close relations with the King's mother, Princess Kossamak, who exercised—and still exercises—considerable influence upon her son.

Finally the Democrats seized upon a technicality to pass a motion of censure against Yem Sambaur. The Premier threatened to request the King to dissolve the Assembly unless the censure motion were withdrawn. The Assembly, however, refused to yield, and Sambaur obtained the King's signature to the dissolution decree. The Assembly thereupon hastily withdrew its censure motion on September 17, 1949, but it was too late. The King, greatly disturbed by the actions of the extremist deputies which threatened the final negotiations for the French-Cambodian treaty, decided that the Assembly had shown itself irresponsible and on September 18 declared that the decree was irrevocable.

This dissolution was entirely legal. What was questionable was the appointment of Yem Sambaur to succeed himself as Premier, since the Constitution provided that in the event of dissolution the President (speaker) of the National Assembly should become the chief executive pending the holding of new elections. The fact that the President of the Assembly, Ieu Koeus (pronounced *Iu Kas*), was shortly thereafter assassinated and that the assassin himself was done away with, accented the worst fears of the Democrats and made for increased underground opposition to the government.

An alarming increase in insurgency throughout the land ensued, and this in turn was used by Yem Sambaur to justify the postponement of elections. There was even reason to believe that Yem Sambaur was in touch with certain rebel groups and induced them to occasional spurts of well-timed activity to reinforce such justification. The Democrats denounced the appointment of Yem Sambaur and the postponement of elections as unconstitutional, but the King's insistence on stable government and his decision to postpone the elections were acceptable to many people who had been dismayed by the irresponsible conduct of various deputies.

The King, in dissolving the Assembly, had publicly declared that he did not intend to depart from legality and from democratic principles, but he was greatly embarrassed by the fact that no Assembly was available to ratify the treaty of 1949 and by the knowledge that the existing Assembly, if he recalled it, would only reject that treaty. He began to consider the possibility of modifying the Constitution, making the Assembly merely a consultative body and shifting the power of ratification to the King alone. Under the Constitution, however, amendments require a three-fourths vote of the Assembly. Since that body had been dissolved, the King appealed to the heads of the political parties. Both Democrats and Liberals strenuously opposed any constitutional changes that would decrease the powers of the Assembly, and the revision project was thus abandoned. As we shall see, this was not the last time that King Sihanouk wanted to circumvent Parliament in amending the Constitution, nor was it the last time when he shrank back from doing this illegally. Even though some of the governments were questionable from a constitutional point of view, the King was always scrupulously concerned to have the form of legality on his side.

In May, 1950 Yem Sambaur's power had become eroded by accusations of corruption, opposition from the French and increasing public insecurity which spread to Phnom Penh itself, where there were student strikes and shootings. The King, as we have already seen in the last chapter, finally sacrificed Sambaur. For a brief time, he headed a government himself. Then there followed an interim government headed by his uncle, Prince Monipong, which included representatives from the Democratic and Liberal parties as well as from all kinds of other parties which had sprung up in the meantime, which claimed to represent wide strata of the country, but whose ballooning influence was subsequently pricked when the next elections were held. Bickering and in-fighting between the political clans—and rivalries, mutual accusations, corrup-

The Agony of Democracy

tion, dissidence, banditry, intrigues, pressure from the French, as well as a three-months' crisis after the fall of Monipong—marked this period until it was finally decided to hold elections again.

As we have seen in the preceding section, in the new elections held in September, 1951 the Democrats repeated their former success by electing fifty-four of their candidates to the seventy-eight-seat Assembly. The Liberal Party again placed second with eighteen; the province of Siemreap (which, as we already know, had become a private fief of Dap Chhuon) elected four deputies on Chhuon's own ticket; and the "Victorious Northeast Khmer Party" and the Khmer Renovation Party elected two. The other grouping, including Yem Sambaur's National Reconstruction Party, elected nobody. Huy Kanthoul became Prime Minister, and immediately a serious deadlock developed in Cambodian-French relations as the Democrats went into almost absolute opposition to the French authorities. Highly-placed Democrats were implicated in the escape of Son Ngoc Thanh and in the ensuing increase of unrest.

The King now insisted that firm measures be taken against the Issaraks, but all the cabinet did by way of maintaining order was to arrest its own political opponents, including the King's friend, Yem Sambaur. This proved too much to King Sihanouk, and on June 15, 1952, he dismissed the government and took over the functions of Prime Minister himself. But he hesitated to dissolve the National Assembly and instead asked it to sanction his extra-constitutional move. The Assembly did not dare to oppose the King overtly but replied that, since he based himself on the principle that all power emanates from the Throne, he was free to do as he pleased—but that the Assembly on its part could not vote him any powers entrusted to it by the people.

It is interesting, both in retrospect and for the perspective it gives on present-day Cambodia, where the situation is in some respects reversed, to cite a few passages of the King's message to the outgoing Huy Kanthoul government. He noted that the government had not followed the lines laid out by him but only "the policy established by the Directing Committee of the Democratic Party.... The Ministers confuse matters of state with party matters as though the interests of their party were *ipso facto* the interests of the state.... Others do not have the right to raise their voice to protest against your injustices. If they do so, you proclaim to the people that they want to betray democracy and overturn the Constitution.... The King himself may have no more security than the others, for already you do not concede him any real authority over the conduct of the nation's affairs on the grounds that you possess that authority by vote of the people—of the people to whom you give the impression that they govern, while you content yourselves to turn their heads with talk about independence but conceal from them the fact that you are letting the country die, that you are delivering it to oppression, pillage and assassination by trouble-makers . . . When I gave the country a Constitution I had the firm conviction that I was transmitting my powers to men who possess real faith in democracy. . . ." The Democrats agreed, of course, that they had not followed the King's policy: It had been their position all along that in a constitutional monarchy the King could reign but must not govern—*i.e.*, that he should stay outside of politics.

Cambodian democracy went completely into abeyance when the King dissolved the second National Assembly in January, 1953. During the period of the "Crusade for Independence," the government was principally conducted by Penn Nouth, with such men as Nhiek Tioulong, Khim Tit, Yem Sambaur, and the ex-Democrats Son Sann and Sim Var in leading positions. The King had declared, when he took over full powers, that he would account for his stewardship within three years, and had sworn "before all the Tevodas and the Most Real Powers that I will allow myself to be arraigned to be judged in public by the people at the expiration of that period." This responsibility he met in a referendum in February, 1955. The question asked was whether the people considered that the King had won the country's independence. The campaign slogan was "*If*

A Short History of Cambodia

you love the King, vote white; if you do not love the King, vote black." The vote was not secret. There were 925,667 white ballots cast and 1,834 black ones.

Under the Geneva agreement, Cambodia undertook to *"take the necessary measures to integrate all citizens, without discrimination, into the national community and to guarantee them the enjoyment of the rights and freedoms for which the Constitution of the Kingdom provides."* It also guaranteed that *"all Cambodian citizens may freely participate as electors or candidates in general elections by secret ballot."* King Sihanouk instituted an interim government to prepare elections and invited all parties, including the Democrats, to participate. The Democratic Party explained that it must first hold a party congress to decide the question, but by the time the congress was held the government of Leng Ngeth (pronounced Leng *Nyet*) was already formed and refused them participation. Nevertheless, the Democratic Party prepared to unlimber its old and tested political machine for the forthcoming political contest.

However, there were no real opponents. The entire political life of the country had become polarized in the last years between the King and his entourage on the one hand and the Democrats on the other. If the King did not step into the electoral arena himself, the Democrats seemed destined to win the elections by simple default as the only party known to the people, and as the party known always to have stood for the country's independence. Petitions began to arrive in the Royal Palace, suggesting that the elections be postponed or altogether canceled. The King was of course delighted with these petitions, and it is not an unreasonable assumption that this delight was in turn communicated to provincial officials. Demonstrations took place, expressing dissatisfaction with the old political system and asking the King himself to take a greater role in the conduct of public affairs.

King Sihanouk convoked two trusted advisors, Sam Sary and Yem Sambaur, to study constitutional means by which the apparent will of the people might be fulfilled. (Yem Sambaur subsequently developed misgivings about the enterprise and did not endorse it.) The result was the King's own proposal for constitutional reform, which he announced in person on Febraury 19, 1955, to the assembled Diplomatic Corps, the Indian, Polish and Canadian heads of the Control Commission, and a mass of Cambodian dignitaries.

The new constitutional reform envisaged doing away with the party system which the King blamed for most of the ills of the country. The King was to appoint the cabinet, and the cabinet was directly responsible to him. There would nevertheless be democracy, only it would be "a democracy that the people could understand." It would be based on the election of local candidates to provincial assemblies and to an Assembly in Phnom Penh, but henceforth the Assembly must not be allowed to overthrow governments and the deputies would have to be residents of the various electoral districts and not, as hitherto, only functionaries living in the capital. Moreover, functionaries as well as deputies should be subject to recall by their constituents. To make sure that the new Assembly be truly representative, the constitutional reform was to provide that all candidates must have been residents for three years in their respective constituencies (which would exclude any Issaraks). The King proposed to hold a referendum on these modifications of the Constitution, and only afterwards the national elections were to be held, to which he had pledged himself to the nation and to the Geneva powers.

Two weeks after he launched this spectacular proposal, King Sihanouk suddenly abdicated. He declared his decision to be irrevocable and designated his parents, Prince Suramarit and Princess Kossamak, to succeed him. He himself, he said, would henceforth go and live, as a humble and poor man, among his people. He had tried to give the people reforms which would allow them to do away with political parties, to be rid of dishonest officials and to change their deputies when these no longer had their confidence, but this reform had encountered "opposition from the politicians, the rich, and the educated, from dishonest people who had carried their complaints to foreigners so that the latter may cause us difficulties by basing their arguments on the false (*i.e.* a false interpretation of the) Geneva agreement."

Although it was at the time a great mystery why the King had abdicated, it now seems that all the answers were contained in his abdication message: his constitutional reform had created dissension even in the supposedly compliant government, and it had met with raised eyebrows from the International Control Commission because the restriction on candidacies (requiring three years of residence in the constituency) seemed to conflict with Article 6 of the Geneva agreement under which Cambodia had undertaken to allow *"all citizens, without discrimination . . . to enjoy the rights and freedoms for which the Constitution of the Kingdom provides."* But if his constitutional reform did not pass before elections were held, the Democrats stood to win again—unless some other way were found to stop them.

Prince Sihanouk, as he was henceforth to be known, found that way. "If I have abdicated," he said, according to a radio broadcast on March 9, "it was not to abandon the people but to save them from the democracy which is pressing upon them, and to obtain the triumph of the new reforms which I have worked out." It soon became apparent that although he had abdicated, the Prince was still in control of the government and overshadowed his parents in importance. The government postponed the elections which had been scheduled for April, and at the beginning of that month there was launched a new political movement, the *"Sangkum Reastr Niyum"* or People's Socialist Community, which was meant to be a vast rally of all right-thinking Cambodians to elect men faithful to the King and the ex-King and to vote, in a legal manner, the constitutional reform worked out by the latter. In other words, the Sangkum was Prince Sihanouk's bid for the three-quarters majority required by the Constitution in order to amend it along the lines he had advocated. The three-year residence requirement and the idea of a referendum were dropped, and the reform proposals were somewhat refined.

The Sangkum proposed to "make the little man King" by making Ministers, deputies and functionaries subject to recall, while making the King, in effect, chief executive and allowing him to fire Ministers and send any dissident deputies back before their electors. The King was to become the "final arbiter of the Constitution" and he alone was to have the right to propose any further amendments to it. Later, when the Sangkum came into power, the features of the reform that dealt with increased powers for the King were dropped and

The Agony of Democracy

only those dealing with checks upon the government and the assembly were enacted.

The Sangkum swept everything before it. It should be emphasized that it did not campaign against democracy—on the contrary, it campaigned in favor of a better kind of democracy, and even today Prince Sihanouk argues that Cambodia has, thanks to his constitutional reforms, more real democracy than any other country. The elections of September, 1955 became, in effect, another referendum on Sihanouk's record in accomplishing his royal mandate. The Prince pictured all his adversaries as disloyal to the monarchy; he campaigned as the liberator of his country and he accused the Democrats of collusion with the Communists, adding the promise that he would rid the country of politicans and overbearing public officials. The full weight of the governmental machinery was deployed in favor of the Sangkum. Criticism of the Prince by the opposition was construed as sedition, and in Phnom Penh a rally of the Democrats was broken up with strong-arm tactics under the eyes of the police. Yet the elections were not unfree. Despite some irregularities, they were certified by the International Control Commission as fulfilling the requirements of the Geneva agreement.

In the elections of September 11, 1955, Prince Sihanouk's Sangkum won 82 percent of the popular vote and 100 percent of the seats in the National Assembly. The Democrats obtained some 12 percent. A new party, the Pracheachon group, which based itself upon the Viet Minh resistance and was obviously the Cambodian equivalent of the Communists, obtained only 3 percent although the geographic distribution of its votes in some of the formerly most guerrilla-ridden areas showed that the Viet Minh still had some courageous sympathizers in places where they could most easily make trouble again some day. The Democratic Party became almost clandestine after the elections, but it was not outlawed. Already infiltrated by leftist elements since its congress in early 1955, it became a secret battleground between those elements on the one hand and the followers of Son Ngoc Thanh and a few moderate old-timers on the other, but the victory of the latter faction did nothing to improve the party's standing with Prince Sihanouk. As a matter of fact, the roots of their controversy lie by now so deep that the Democrats and the Sangkum hate and fear each other far more than either of them hates or fears the Communists. This, as we shall see in the next section, has had an indirect effect upon Cambodian foreign policy.

The Sangkum has been in power since September, 1955, and its power has been uncontested and Sihanouk's leadership unchallenged. He is the leader of the country, whether he exercises the func-

The Agony of Democracy.

tions of Prime Minister, which he has done occasionally, or whether he merely lives in his retreat at Siemreap, where the government submits to him all important decisions and even many unimportant ones. He controls the Sangkum, the Parliament, the Government, and exercises predominant influence upon his parents, the King and Queen. He has instituted new economic and social measures and extended his constitutional reform by creating "national congresses" where, theoretically, anybody can speak up and debate the issues of the day.*

The Sangkum governments have not been free from factionalism, rivalries and corruption, and the inexperience of Cambodian politicians, which in large measure is traceable to their fundamental lack of education, has plagued the Sangkum almost as much as it had plagued the Democrats. Even the National Assembly has occasionally made trouble for the government, as it did in the bygone days of party rule. But these internal stresses and adjustments have been relatively unimportant compared

---

* New elections were held in Cambodia on March 23, 1958. Prince Sihanouk's Sangkum obtained 99.96 percent of the vote and again, of course, all seats in the National Assembly. (Only one seat was contested, by the Pracheachon group which obtained no more than 396 votes.) The Democratic Party, virtually defunct since some of its members suffered violence in August, 1957, did not participate in the elections. However, an increasing number of former Democrats had come to heed Prince Sihanouk's appeal for cooperation within the Sangkum, and a few of them were allowed to run on the Sangkum ticket and thus were among those elected.

with the questions of foreign policy that have arisen since Cambodia obtained its independence. The main weight of Prince Sihanouk's activities since the Sangkum came to power has been on the international scene.

7.

Cambodia in the World Today

CAMBODIAN attitudes in foreign affairs are, like attitudes generally anywhere, largely the result of past experiences and conditioning. It is therefore helpful to pass some of those experiences in review before describing the peculiar way in which Cambodia's foreign policy has developed since the country became independent in 1953. As we have seen, the hatred of Viet Nam goes back over many centuries, during which Annam annexed large parts of Cambodian territory. Thus Cambodians, in their fight against the Viet Minh, hated those rivals and adversaries far more as Vietnamese than as Communists. The Viet Minh invasion of Cambodia in 1954 further heightened such feelings and reinforced the view of Communism as a Vietnamese slogan. There was thus little awareness of the international nature of the Communist conspiracy. The propaganda themes heard in France and also in America, to the effect that the war in Indochina was the result of Communist aggression, had little plausibility in Cambodia, which felt that it was fighting for its freedom both against the Vietnamese and against the French, with Communism a mere side-issue. While Cambodia emerged from the war with ample reason to fear Communist North Viet Nam, the traditional hatred and suspicion of the Annamites extended as much to anti-Communist South Viet Nam as it did to the North.

As regards Cambodia's other major neighbor, Thailand, sentiment was naturally inflamed by the renewed rape of the western provinces during the Japanese occupation. Thai support for Cambodian dissidents, moreover, had not gone unnoticed by King Sihanouk, and his treatment in Bangkok when he had tried to exile himself there during his "Crusade for Independence"—he was treated as a political refugee rather than as a reigning monarch— was probably also not forgotten. (The third neighbor, Laos, which has only a relatively short common boundary, presented an anomaly: although Cambodia established diplomatic relations with many exceedingly distant countries with which it had no common problems and interests, no diplomatic missions were for many years exchanged with Laos, probably because of a feeling of disdain for a still smaller, weaker and more backward country. But there was no animosity toward Laos.)

There is no need to dwell at length upon the well-known phenomenon of heightened nationalism on the part of a country recently emerged from a status of dependence upon a European colonial power. It should be stressed, however, that after Cambodia obtained its independence, relations with France improved to the point where they could be termed cordial. Many French advisers remained in the government, and French soldiers continued to train the Cambodian army, if only for the simple reason that Cambodian officers spoke French. The cultural influence of France is still considerable. This cultural influence has, in fact, left a peculiar political heritage. As mentioned earlier, most French administrators in Indochina tended to the Right, but most French schoolteachers, of whom there still are many in Cambodia, have tended consistently to the Left, as they do in France, and they have left a certain imprint of Marxist thinking upon their charges. To this has been added the ideological baggage acquired by Cambodian students in France, whose numbers increased after World War II. Many of these young men returned with leftist and neutralist views current in French intellectual circles, and some returned as Communist agents. But even the extreme Left in Cambodia manifested itself more in propaganda against American "imperialism" and in favor of "peace" and neutrality, than in any advocacy of Communism. In a country which has no industrial proletariat, no land problem and (despite a very low standard of living) little grinding poverty, the appeal of outright Communist doctrine is in any event limited.

Cambodia's attitude toward her neighbors is well illustrated by a comment of Royal High Councillor Sam Sary in his book "Bilan de l'Oeuvre de Norodom Sihanouk," in which he discussed the accomplishments of Cambodian diplomacy, notably the establishment of relations with some forty-three countries in the period between 1950 and 1954: "Some may ask," he wrote, "why Cambodia has not yet concluded any agreement to improve economic and financial cooperation either with France or with the neighboring countries. . . . The principal reason is that the full independence and sovereignty which Cambodia enjoys today might suffer a diminution, however slight, if any agreement were to be concluded. For any international agreement is in fact a compromise resulting from reciprocal concessions. Such concessions entail advantages, to be sure, but they also entail a surrender of advantages to the other side." No one could have expressed in clearer terms the nationalist reluctance of Cambodia to enter into any international arrangements. The fact that Thailand, for instance, became a member of SEATO was interpreted in Cambodia as evidence that it had traded part of its independence for American protection. A similar attitude existed with respect to South Viet Nam, which was suspected of having alienated part of its sovereignty by lining up too clearly on the side of the West.

Yet Cambodia did not become anti-Western in the course of its struggle against French rule. There was sufficient awareness of Communist support for the Viet Minh to make responsible Cambodians, including the freedom fighters, look to the West for support both in attaining their freedom and defending it. Even Son Ngoc Thanh called upon France to "follow the British and American examples" and some of his propaganda promised that once he had obtained independence, Cambodia would "gladly enter into the bloc of the democratic countries." King Sihanouk used similar arguments in his famous letter to President Auriol, letting it be understood for instance that a liberated Cambodia might develop a relationship to France similar to that between the liberated Philippines and the United States.

When he published in 1953 a "Yellow Book" on the Cambodian struggle for freedom, the King included in its preface the sentence: "To the American people, this book confirms that the eyes of the countries aspiring to independence turn hopefully to their glorious and mighty country, knowing that many peoples owe to it their freedom and even their very existence." It was no secret from Sihanouk that the United States, even while supporting the French struggle against Communism in Indochina, had consistently supported and enhanced the international personality of Cambodia: as early as 1951, the U.S. concluded economic and military assistance agreements with Cambodia, although for some years afterwards the aid was still administered in Saigon and conveyed to Cambodia through the French. An American Ambassador arrived in Phnom Penh only after Geneva.

At the conference in Geneva, Cambodia astounded the world with its almost impertinent opposition to the Communist powers. Although the entire conference was prepared to write into the Cambodian agreement restrictions similar to those in the agreements on Laos and Viet Nam, and although Prime Minister Mendès-France had staked his political future on his ability to come up with an agreement by midnight of July 20, 1954, the Cambodian delegation refused to budge: under the leadership of Tep Phan, Sam Sary, and Nong Kimny, the delegation was unperturbed by threats from Molotov and insisted that it could not sign an agreement that barred it from concluding any military alliance or from authorizing the establishment of foreign military bases or from soliciting foreign military assistance. Cambodia was willing to guarantee unilaterally that it would be neutral and that its army would not exceed a certain size, but it could accept no foreign-imposed limitation upon its sovereignty. As a result of this intransigence, Cambodia won virtually all its points: the agreement as finally signed barred it from contracting military alliances only if they are *"not in conformity with the United Nations Charter"*; from permitting foreign military bases only *"as long as its security is not threatened"*; and from soliciting foreign military assistance *"except for the purpose of effective defense of the territory."* Cambodia had retained its freedom of action although, as events were to show, it had no intention of using it by joining any collective defense arrangement.

Almost immediately upon his abdication as King, Prince Sihanouk paid a visit to Prime Minister Nehru in New Delhi. Relations between the two had not been particularly good, since Nehru had been inclined to see in Son Ngoc Thanh a more ardent nationalist than the King and had even met with the former resistance leader in October 1954. The meeting between Nehru and the ex-King, however, was a complete success. Prince Sihanouk was favorably disposed toward Nehru's neutrality and embraced without hesitation the innocuous sentiments about mutual respect, non-interference, non-aggression, equality, etc. which Nehru and Chou En-Lai had codified in the "Five Principles of Co-existence." The joint communiqué referred to the "historical connections and close cultural affinity between India and Cambodia which date back to a remote past . . . [and] have enabled the leader of the Cambodian Delegation and the Prime Minister of India to understand and appreciate each other's point of view." Prince Sihanouk also led the Cambodian delegation to the Bandung Conference of African and Asian countries and there again proclaimed his adherence to a policy of neutrality, *i.e.* of friendly relations with both East and West and non- involvement in their conflicts. This policy won the enthusiastic endorsement even of the Democrats who had always suspected Sihanouk of excessive subservience to foreigners.

Yet Prince Sihanouk was quite aware that even a neutral Cambodia required means to defend itself, and, after having been spoon-fed American military aid through the French, he was particularly anxious to enter into a relationship with the United States by which his country could receive military equipment and financial support directly. An agreement to that effect was negotiated in early 1955 by the Leng Ngeth government, with Royal High Councillor Sam Sary as the principal Cambodian negotiator. The Democrats immediately claimed, however, that such negotiations exceeded the competence of the Leng Ngeth government, which had been established for the purpose of preparing the elections, and they demanded, unsuccessfully, to be included in the negotiations.

The opposition was not against American military aid, but it felt that the government could not be trusted to obtain it without some secret surrenders of sovereignty. When the agreement was finally published, the electoral campaign was in full swing, and particularly the left-wingers among the Democrats seized upon it as an issue that tied in well with their hyper-nationalist propaganda. The Indian delegation of the International Control Commission also examined the agreement with great suspicion, although finally the ICC declared that its implementation would not conflict with the Geneva agreement. However, Prince Sihanouk found himself in the unenviable position of having to defend a basically unpopular act of the government and he confined himself to claiming that he had had nothing to do with the negotiations, although the agreement did not seem dangerous to him. In addition, he promised to submit the general question of foreign aid again to the people.

The Prince's failure to come out vigorously in defense of the aid agreement and the general queasiness of the government on the subject can now be recognized as the result of its failure to consult with the opposition, which had thus been handed a propaganda issue. The Prince and his

Sangkum were henceforth particularly anxious to demonstrate that they had in no way bargained away any advantage to the Americans, and this anxiousness produced an occasional truculence and a desire to prove that Cambodia, even though it received both military and economic aid from the United States, was "truly neutral." A national congress, convoked at the end of 1955 to re-examine the question of American military aid, confined itself to declaring that Cambodia would accept aid "from any quarter, provided it does not prejudice its independence, sovereignty and neutrality." Although Cambodia had only recently, in August, 1955, been frightened by reports of Viet Minh activities on its northeastern frontier, the Prince felt it wise to establish direct contact with the Communist powers as a demonsration of his independence. The Indian government also encouraged him strongly in that direction.

    Opportunities for Prince Sihanouk to demonstrate his independence in foreign affairs were not lacking. He went to Manila, where he pointedly refused to make any statement which might be even remotely construed as favoring collective defense under SEATO. He was, in fact, rather annoyed by the plain talk of the Philippine leaders, to which he was quite unaccustomed, since even the French had always treated him with extraordinary deference while in his own country, of course, and he had become the subject of truly oriental adulation and flattery. The bluff friendliness of the Philippine leaders, who did not hesitate to talk about the advantages of a policy different from his own, proved particularly jarring in comparison with his next hosts: Mao Tse-Tung and Chou En-Lai. The Chinese Communists were delighted with Cambodia's decision to be neutral and congratulated Prince Sihanouk on his far-sighted statesmanship and moral courage. They spoke of peace and coexistence, offered economic assistance to Cambodia and let it be understood that if ever the Prince had trouble with the Viet Minh, he need only to appeal to Peking to have it stopped. Prince Sihanouk returned to Phnom Penh with the feeling that he had won new friends who might prove useful in counterbalancing any tendency of his old friends to take his reliance upon them for granted.

Shortly thereafter, a crisis occurred in the relations between Cambodia and the United States. Although the differences have long since been settled, the origin and nature of that crisis are of great interest to the student of Cambodian history because almost all the elements that have been hitherto discussed were present: hatred of the Annamites, fear of Thailand, the heritage of internal conflict over the independence issue, neutrality, the peculiar Cambodian conception of collective security, nationalism, and Prince Sihanouk's extraordinary sensitivity plus his shrewd political sense and leadership qualities.

Upon his return from Peking in February, 1956, Prince Sihanouk learned a number of things. South Viet Nam had suddenly imposed a stoppage on all trade with Cambodia. Although no public explanation has been offered, it was clear that President Diem had become annoyed by a Cambodian press campaign which accused the Vietnamese government of border violations (that had been patently the result of rebel activities along the border) and which revived the Cambodian claims to Cochinchina (*i.e.*, one-half of South Viet Nam). The history of these differences was long and involved, and although Prince Sihanouk had himself started the new controversy with a press interview in France earlier that year, he thought he was placing the matter in proper context when he also learned that "American aid imports had been stopped." (Actually, some frauds had been discovered and the Cambodian government itself had suspended the imports temporarily.) He also heard, quite correctly, that United States representatives were displeased with statements he had made earlier, in which he had disparaged American aid to Cambodia in comparing it with aid given to the Philippines. The Prince was returning triumphantly from his trip to China and feared that he was being confronted with American sanctions motivated by his flirtation with the Communists. In a speech to the National Assembly on February 29, he complained that "the United States wants only to help the countries which accept its supervision" and contrasted this with an offer of aid "without any condition" which he had just received from Chou En-Lai.

In the same speech, which gave signs of having been written in great haste and nervousness, Prince Sihanouk restated at length his territorial claims on South Viet Nam, which was hardly calculated to improve his relations with that country. He also said: "The Americans are dissatisfied because I have refused the proposals of the Philippines to adhere to SEATO and because I have declared that American aid is used for enriching those who are already rich... If the Americans want to cut off their aid to Cambodia, we on our part are resolved to remain faithful to our neutrality policy. We will accept neither Soviet nor Chinese aid." However, he also said: "We can assume that, if we ask for economic aid from a foreign country, several nations will hasten to reply to our appeal... If our domestic and foreign policies are well balanced, our country will have full foreign aid like India, and our national sovereignty will be strengthened. We will accept aid from the right, from the left and from the center in any way which will stabilize our policy." In other words, Prince Sihanouk was complaining of alleged American pressure. He feared that American aid was being cut off; and he declared that he could not rely on Communist aid alone, but he desired to receive Communist aid precisely because he felt it would counter-balance American aid and make the country less vulnerable to pressure from any quarter.

The diplomatic aspects of the crisis were complex and cannot be discussed in detail. As often happens in diplomatic crises, entirely unrelated matters were suddenly related to it and there ensued a snowball effect which magnified the differences and inflamed the passions. Soon spontaneous demonstrations were taking place throughout Cambodia, recalling the similar allegedly spontaneous but well-organized demonstrations that had called upon the King to postpone the 1955 elections. Well-lettered placards and banners were carried, protesting against "foreign pressure against Cambodian neutrality" and implying that the United States was deliberately delaying construction of a new road to the sea, presumably in order to allow the Vietnamese better to strangle Cambodia. (The placards read: *"If the foreigners do not build the road to Kompong Som, we shall do so with our own hands."*) The fact that the United States was giving its support to the Cambodian military budget in goods rather than in cash was suddenly pictured as an insult (because South Viet Nam was known to receive cash). But the element that aroused Prince Sihanouk to greatest passion, because it seemed to bring proof of a concerted campaign of "pressure against Cambodian neutrality," was a declaration by Prime Minister Pibulsonggram of Thailand that his government was considering closing its border with Cambodia.

Only by bearing in mind what we have learned about Cambodian attitudes toward Viet Nam and Thailand, about neutrality as an expression of sovereignty, and about the interpretation of alignment with the West as a surrender of one's independence, can one begin to understand why Cambodia's leader did not hesitate to ascribe to the United States his difficulties with his neighbors, whose friendship he had done nothing to obtain even while he had gone to fraternize with their mortal enemy. Indian diplomacy, which is motivated by similar attitudes, did not scruple to support Prince Sihanouk in his interpretation of what was happening, and it, too, was doubtless acting in good faith.

Any news that came to hand was used to support and build up the campaign about American, rather than Vietnamese, pressure. If an American magazine printed a snide and malicious article on Prince Sihanouk, this was interpreted as more evidence of the American master mind at work. If, on the other hand, the United States was patiently laboring to compose the differences with Viet Nam and to prevent the closing of the Thai frontier, this was interpreted as proof that the U.S. was indeed pulling the wires of power and policy in those two countries. "In any case," declared Prince Sihanouk in a speech at Kampot on April 6, 1956, "the Americans, who have so often promised to defend the freedom of little countries, have just shown their true face to Cambodia. It is not a noble one." In the same speech, however, he declared that Cambodia was unable to do without American military aid, even though it was being given in a "humiliating" manner. "If we tried to do without American aid," he said, "we would fall into the Communist orbit, which would be the end of our neutrality and probably of our independence."

The accusations against the United States were so utterly fantastic and unfair that tempers ran exceedingly high. Although the episode served further to reinforce the peculiar Cambodian conception of neutrality, it did not lastingly impair relations between the United States and Cambodia, since those relations are based less on sentiment than on a mutual interest in maintaining Cambodia's independence. For that reason, no consideration was given to stopping American aid even though the instinctive reaction of patriotic Americans must have been to do so—and even though Prince Sihanouk himself kept saying (and believing) that the United States was threatening to cut off its aid.

It will come as no surprise to readers of the preceding two chapters that Prince Sihanouk's rampage brought him the unanimous support of the

Cambodia Today

opposition parties, ranging from the Communists all the way to the right-wing Democrats. Never, in fact, did Prince Sihanouk have a more united country behind him than when he stood up against both its hated neighbors and against seeming pressure by their mighty protector, standing them all off in the name of Cambodian neutrality and sovereignty and in the name of a peaceful policy of equal friendship and equal aid from East and West. The danger of Communism, which had never been greatly feared, was temporarily altogether forgotten.

Later in 1956 the Prince went to Moscow, Warsaw, and Prague (he also visited Austria, Spain, and Sweden), again endorsed the "Five Principles of Coexistence" and for a time seemed completely taken in by the Communist protestations of friendship and sympathy. However, the Prince was merely trying to gather up weights to cast into the balance, and he was well aware that his balancing act between East and West could only succeed if the United States did not remove its own weight from the other side of the scales. Gradually, this realization became an obsession, and as a strange result of this now almost-forgotten crisis there remained behind an improved and increased appreciation of American economic and military aid as indeed essential for the maintenance of Cambodia's independence.

Cambodia thus remains poised between East and West, but despite the self-satisfaction over its balancing act, it cannot help looking down occasionally into the abyss below. Gradually it is being brought home to Cambodian leaders that there is a difference in kind between aid from America, a faraway country which can obtain no possible commensurate advantages in Cambodia, and aid from Communist China which has the capability of mobilizing a minority of 250,000 of its nationals inside Cambodia and which can act at any time to call out the guerrillas who once fought under orders from North Vietnam, which in turn can mobilize some of its 300,000 compatriots in the country. In the beginning of 1957 the Prince called yet another national congress to consider this question, among other issues. That body obediently produced a resolution which spoke of Cambodian neutrality, reiterated the country's determination to remain aloof from any military or ideological alliance, protested its own peaceful intentions, and added that Cambodia would attempt to defend itself if it were to be attacked. In the case of such an attack, the resolution went on, Cambodia would first appeal to the United Nations. But if the UN were to prove unable to send immediate help, the resolution concluded, Cambodia would seek the intervention of " a friendly power."

Although diplomatically worded, this meant that if the Communists were to make any serious trouble for Cambodia, Prince Sihanouk would waste

Cambodia Today

little time in seeking Western help—perhaps even if this entailed assistance also by Cambodia's anti-Communist neighbors, by the descendants of the hated Annamites and by the Thais, the conquerors of Angkor.

Bibliography

Etienne-François Aymonier, *Le Cambodge*; Paris, E. Leroux, 1900.

Adhémard Leclère, *Histoire du Cambodge;* Paris, P. Geuthner, 1914.

Georges Maspéro, *Le Royaume du Champa*; Paris, G. van Oest, 1928.

H. Marchal, *Guide Archéologique aux Temples d'Angkor*; Paris, G. van Oest, 1928.

G. Coedès, *Pour mieux comprendre Angkor*; Hanoi, Imprimerie d'Extrème Orient, 1943.

Henri Russier, *Histoire sommaire du royaume du Cambodge*; Hanoi, Imprimerie d'Extrème Orient, 1944.

Maurice Glaize, *Les monuments du groupe d'Angkor*; Saigon, Albert Portail, 1944.

G. Coedès, *Histoire ancienne des états hindouisés d'Extrème Orient*; Hanoi, Imprimerie d'Extrème Orient, 1944.

Office Français d'Edition, *Angkor, la resurrection de l'art Khmer et l'oeuvre de l'école française d'Extrème Orient*; Paris, Office Français d'Edition.

Henri Parmentier, *Angkor* (A Guidebook); Saigon, Albert Portail, 1950.

Lawrence P. Briggs, *The Ancient Khmer Empire*; Philadelphia, American Philosophic Society, 1951.

Chou Ta-kuan, *Mémoires sur les coutumes du Cam-*

bodge (P. Pelliot); Paris, Librairie de l'Amérique et d'Orient, 1951.

Gouvernement Royal du Cambodge, *Livre Jaune sur les revendications de l'indépendance du Cambodge;* Paris, Imprimerie Centrale Commerciale, 1954.

Reginald le May, *The Culture of Southeast Asia*; London, George Allen & Unwin, 1954.

Sam Sary, *La grande figure de Norodom Sihanouk;* Phnom Penh, Imprimerie du Palais Royal, 1955.

Sam Sary and Mau Say, *Bilan de l'Oeuvre de Norodom Sihanouk*; Phnom Penh, Imprimerie Albert Portail, 1955.

Bernard-Philippe Groslier, *The Arts and Civilization of Angkor;* New York, Frederick A. Praeger, 1957.

Index

Ang Chan (King), 44, 51, 52
Ang Duong (King), 52, 53, 54, 55, 57
Ang Em (Prince), 48, 52, 54, 55
Angkor, 8, 9, 11, 14, 15, 18, 19, 20, 21-22, 23, 25, 27, 28, 29, 33, 37, 39, 40, 43, 44, 47, 50, 51, 52, 63, 135
Angkor Thom, 11, 12, 15, 19, 22, 23, 26, 28, 32
Angkor Wat, 16, 21, 22, 47, 74
Ang Mey (Queen), 51
Ang Non II, 48
Attlee, Clement, 77
Auriol, Vincent, 89, 90, 91, 121
Ayuthia, 15, 37, 44, 46, 50

Bali, 43
Bandung, 124
Bangkok, 46, 50, 55, 58, 59, 87, 92, 118
Bao Dai (Emperor), 75, 79, 91
Banteay Srei, 13, 23
Barom Racha (King), 44
Battambang, 58, 61, 62, 66, 92
Bouillevaux, Abbé, 32
Briggs, Lawrence P., 9, 18

Cap Varella, 44
Chadomuk, 15
Champa, 11, 28, 32, 35, 40, 41, 42, 43, 44, 45, 52
Chams, 20, 27, 40, 43, 47

Chey Chettah (King), 45
Chey Chettah II, 47
Chey Chettah IV, 48, 49, 50, 51
Chhuon Mochulpich, 83, 105
Chhean Vam, 100
Chiang Kai-shek, 77
Chou En-Lai, 123, 127, 129
Chou Ta-Kuan, 19, 28, 29, 30, 31, 32, 35, 36, 37

Dap Chhuon; *see* Chhuon Mochulpich
De Lagrée, Doudart, 58
De Langlade, General, 88

Ea Sichau, 84
Eintapath, 12

Finot, Louis, 17, 20
Funan, 8

Geneva, 93, 94, 108, 110, 111, 122, 125
Gia-Long (Emperor), 51
Giang, General; *see* Truon-minh-Giang

Haiphong, 77
Hanoi, 67, 68, 70, 77
Ha Tien, 49
Hem Cheao, 74
Ho Chi Minh, 77
Huy Kanthoul, 105, 106

Index

Ieu Koeus, 102
Indrapura, 43
Indravarman III, 13, 14, 29, 30, 31

Jayavarman II, 40
Jayavarman VII, 15, 27
Jayavarman VIII, 13, 14, 15

Kambujadesa, 37
Kampot, 132
Kaundinya, 8
Khim Tit, 64, 100, 107
Khmer Issarak, 78, 79, 80, 81, 82, 83, 84, 85, 86, 87, 88, 89, 90, 105
Khublai Khan, 28
Kompong Som, 130
Kossamak (Princess, Queen), 102, 110, 115

La Napoule, 88
Leclerc, General, 75
Leclère, Adhemard, 14, 16, 20, 47
Leng Ngeth, 108, 124
Letourneau, Jean, 87
Lovek, 15, 20, 44, 45, 46

Manila, 126
Mao Tse-Tung, 127
Marco Polo, 42
Mendès-France, Pierre, 122
Molotov, Vyacheslav, 122
Monipong (Prince), 104, 105
Monireth (Prince), 65, 99
Monivong (King), 64
Moscow, 133

Mouhaut, Henri, 23
Murray, Brigadier, 75

Napoleon III, 58, 59, 60
Nehru, Jawaharlal, 123, 124
New Delhi, 123
New York, 91
Ngo-dinh-Diem, 128
Nong Kimny, 122
Norodom (King), 57, 58, 59, 60, 61, 64, 65, 73

Ottawa, 91
Outey, 47

Pach Chhoeun, 74, 75, 78
Paris, 59, 90
Peking, 127, 128
Penn Nouth, 89, 93, 101, 107
Phnom Koulen, 26
Phnom Penh, 7, 10, 15, 22, 43, 48, 54, 63, 64, 66, 76, 83, 87, 88, 91, 92, 93, 94, 98, 104, 110, 113, 122, 127
Pibulsonggram, Marshal, 131
Pochentong, 83
Ponha To, 47
Ponha Yat, 37
Prague, 133
Pursat, 15, 52

Russier, Henri, 45

Saigon, 41, 47, 48, 49, 51, 52, 55, 58, 70, 76, 77, 122
Sam Sary, 89, 109, 120, 122, 124
Senaka (King), 11

140

Index

Siemreap, 61, 62, 83, 105, 115
Sihanu (King), 11, 12, 13, 14
Sihanouk, Norodom (King), 75, 76, 77, 80, 81, 82, 83, 84, 85, 86, 87, 88, 89, 90, 91, 92, 93, 94, 95, 97, 99, 101, 102, 103, 104, 105, 106, 107, 108, 109, 110, 111, 118, 119, 120, 121, 122
Sihanouk, Norodom (as Prince), 65, 111, 112, 113, 114, 115, 116, 123, 124, 125, 126, 127, 128, 129, 130, 131, 132, 133
Sim Var, 107
Sisophon, 51, 61, 62
Sisowath (King), 60, 64, 65
Sivotha (Prince), 58, 59
Son Ngoc Minh, 85, 94
Son Ngoc Thanh, 73, 74, 75, 76, 77, 83, 84, 85, 86, 90, 91, 94, 105, 114, 121, 123
Son Sann 67, 107
Sonn Voeunsai, 67
Soriyopor (King), 46
Sotha I, 45
Stalin, Josef, 77
Suramarit (Prince, later King), 110
Svay Rieng, 7

Ta Prohm, 23, 27
T-Chay, 12, 13, 14, 16
Tep Phan, 122
Thomma Racha II, 49
Timur Khan, 28
Tioulong, Nhiek, 100, 107
Tokyo, 92
Tonle Sap, 9, 101
Truman, Harry S., 77
Truon-minh Giang, 51

Udong, 15, 48, 52, 53, 54, 55, 58, 63

Viet Minh, 79, 81, 82, 84, 85, 87, 88, 91, 92, 93, 94, 114, 117, 121, 126, 127
Vijaya, 43, 44

Warsaw, 133

Yem Sambaur, 80, 81, 82, 101, 102, 103, 104, 105, 107, 109
Yutevong (Prince), 98, 99

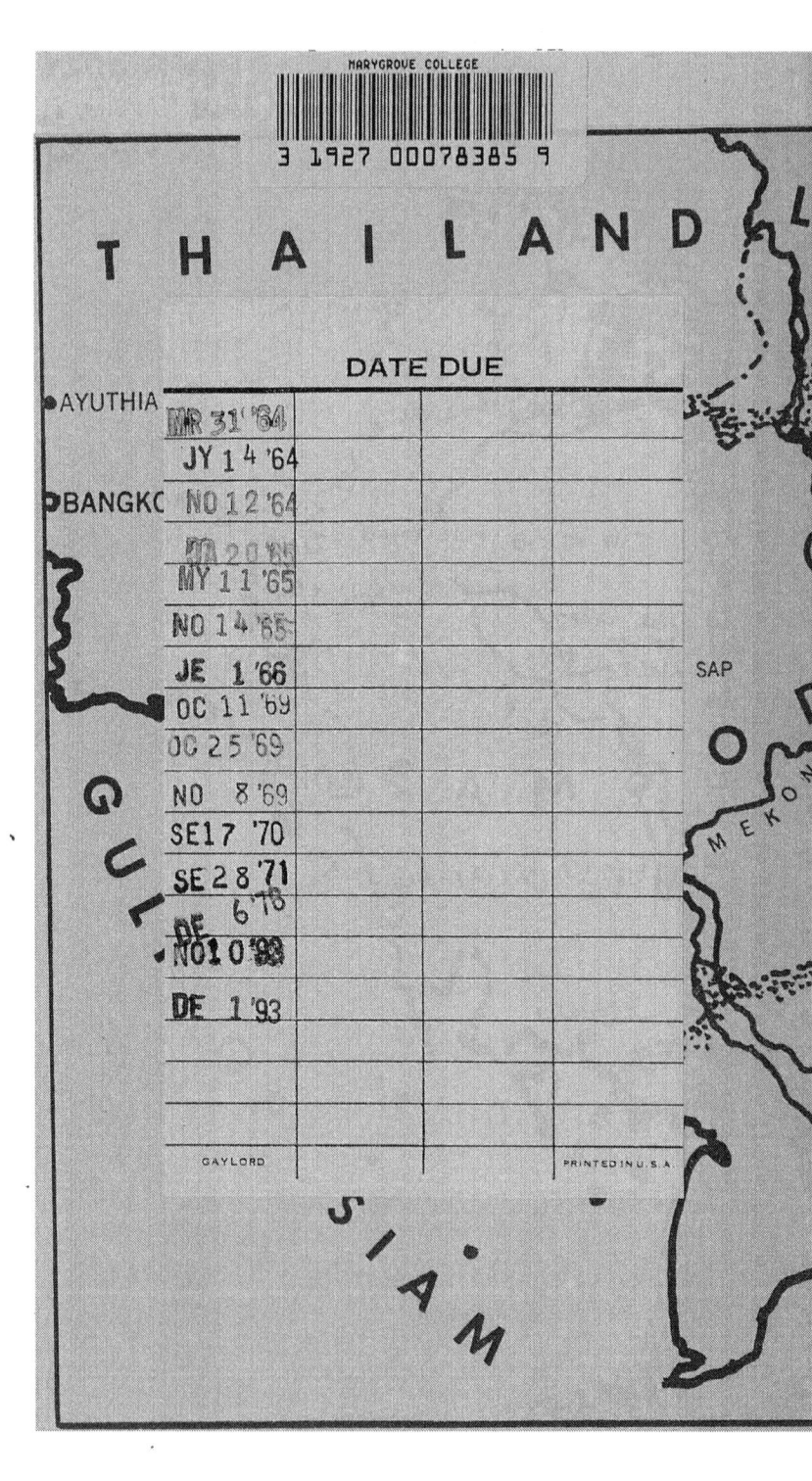

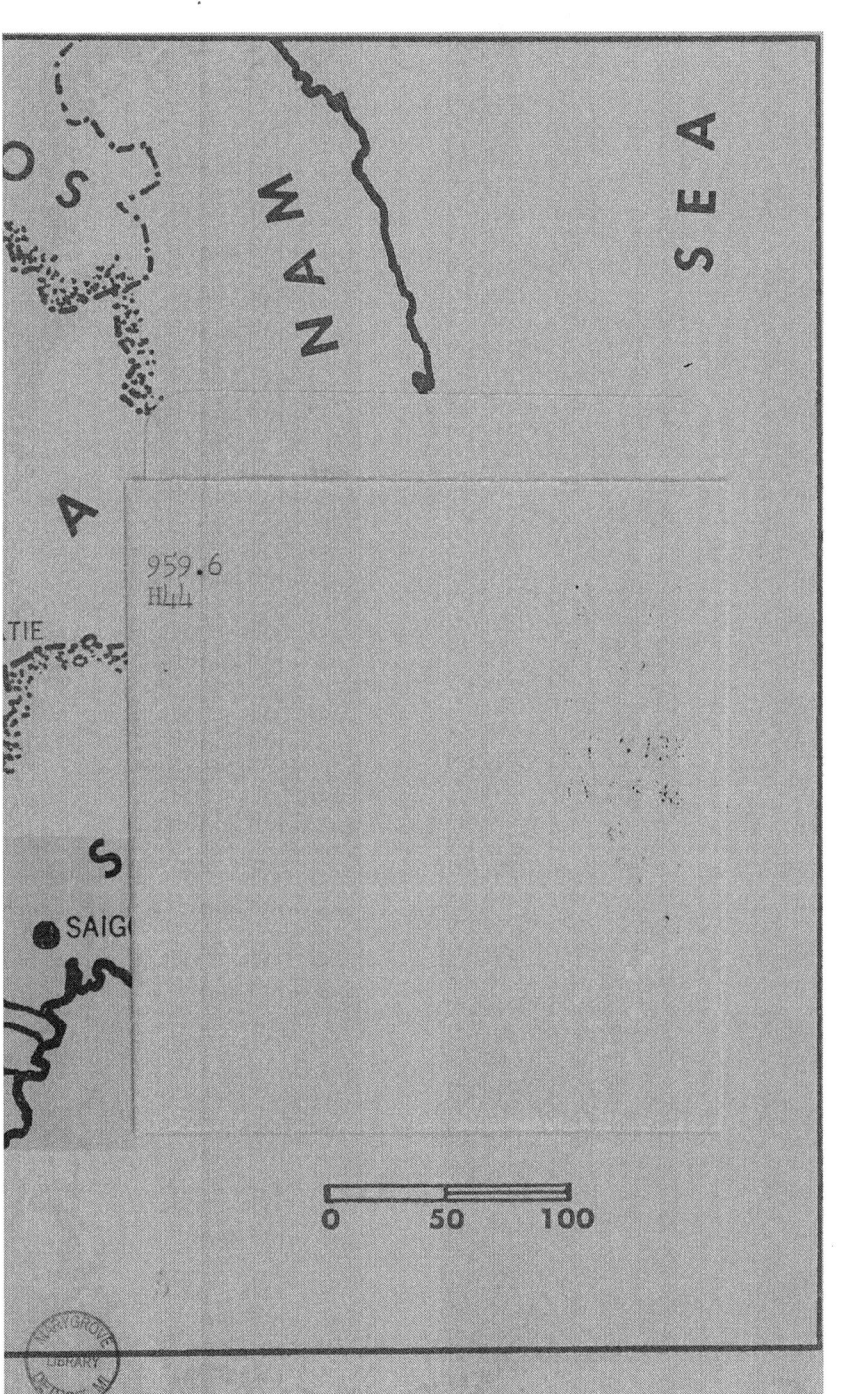

Printed in the USA
CPSIA information can be obtained
at www.ICGtesting.com
CBHW052332011224
18292CB00013B/1150